DISCOVERING JESUS

A 40-DAY BIBLE STUDY THROUGH SCRIPTURE
TO KNOW THE SON OF GOD

40-DAY BIBLE STUDY SERIES

PETER DEHAAN

Books in the 40-Day Bible Study Series:

- Dear Theophilus (the Gospel of Luke)
- Acts Bible Study
- Isaiah Bible Study
- Minor Prophets Bible Study
- Job Bible Study
- Living Water (John)
- Love Is Patient (1 and 2 Corinthians)
- Revelation Bible Study
- 1, 2, & 3 John Bible Study
- Hebrews Bible Study
- James and Jude Bible Study
- Matthew Bible Study
- 1 & 2 Peter Bible Study
- Mark Bible Study
- Romans Bible Study
- Paul's Short Epistles Bible Study

CONTENTS

DISCOVERING JESUS

Jesus is the star of the Bible. The Old Testament points to him and the New Testament reveals him.

Jesus is also the theme for this collection of Bible studies. They're selected from books in the 40-Day Bible Study Series. The forty lessons are grouped into eight weeks. For personal study, consider reading one lesson a day for forty days. For group study, you may want to go at a slower pace, reading five lessons a week, Monday through Friday, for eight weeks.

Like the Bible, this book will point you to Jesus and tell you about him, all through the lens of Scripture. In doing so you can grow closer to knowing the Son of God.

May the Holy Spirit speak to you as you read each day's lesson. As you do, may you love Jesus more fully and impact the world around you for his Father's glory.

[If you're not that familiar with the Bible or want to learn more, check out the appendix "About the Bible" for helpful information and background.]

WEEK 1: THE PROMISED WORD

DAY 1: JESUS: THE WORD, THE LIFE, AND THE LIGHT

JOHN 1:1–14

In him was life, and that life was the light of all mankind.
(John 1:4)

The book of John opens with a most moving passage. It's lyrical, it's evocative, and it is exquisite.

In this poetic prelude of John's Gospel, he calls Jesus the Word, and asserts that the Word *is* God. This means Jesus is God. While some people may think it's an overreach to claim that the Word refers to Jesus, keep reading.

To remove all doubt, John later states that this Word becomes human to join us on earth. Jesus becomes a man to live among us. Jesus, as the Word, shows us his glory as the one and only Son from Father God. Jesus overflows with grace and abounds in truth. He is the Word sent to us from God.

We often assume the Word of God means Scripture. But remember that the New Testament of the Bible didn't exist until several centuries after Jesus's death and resurrection. Because of this, we should consider God's Word as his *spoken* Word, more so than his *written* Word. What if Jesus is more than the metaphorical Word? What if he serves as the actual Word of God? Yes, Jesus is the Word.

John also writes that in Jesus is life. Jesus is present when time begins and takes part in forming our existence. In fact, without Jesus, creation cannot occur. Physical life flows through Jesus at creation. In the same way, eternal life emanates through Jesus now. Jesus comes so we may have life and live with abundance (John 10:10). This theme of life recurs throughout the book of John, with his writing mentioning life in forty-one verses, more often than any other book in the Bible.

The life *of* Jesus, and the life *through* Jesus, gives us light. Just as the sun that Jesus created illuminates our physical world, the light that Jesus gives off now illuminates our spiritual world. This light shines for us in the darkness that surrounds us, exposing the evil in our world. Best of all, this light of Jesus overcomes the darkness, pushing it away. This means good is stronger than evil. God is more powerful than Satan. Hold on to this truth. Don't forget it.

Jesus is the light. As the light—our true light—he comes into our world to save us. Though many do not recognize him or accept him, everyone who receives him and believes in his name become children of God, born of God.

Because of Jesus we've been born into the physical realm, and through our belief in him we are born a second time into the spiritual realm.

Take time to contemplate John's profound opening to his biography, revealing Jesus as the Word, the life, and the light.

Do you recognize Jesus as Word, life, and light? Do you believe in him?

[Discover what else John says about the Word of

God in 1 John 2:14, Revelation 1:1–2, Revelation 19:12–13, and Revelation 20:4.]

Today's reading comes from *Living Water: 40 Reflections on Jesus's Life and Love from the Gospel of John.*

DAY 2: A CHILD IS BORN
ISAIAH 9

For to us a child is born, to us a son is given, and the government will be on his shoulders. And he will be called Wonderful Counselor, Mighty God, Everlasting Father, Prince of Peace. (Isaiah 9:6)

The book of Isaiah contains many prophecies that look forward to Jesus, the people's promised and much-anticipated coming King. In what may be the best known of these prophecies, Isaiah gives us amazing and comforting characteristics about our future Savior, Jesus.

Isaiah starts by saying that Jesus will come as a child, God's gift to us. Father God will send Jesus to us as an infant, who will grow up to become our supreme ruler for the rest of time.

Though Isaiah doesn't specifically call him *Jesus*, the prophet does give us four other awesome names.

First, we'll call him *Wonderful Counselor*. Though anyone can give advice, not all advice is good, and some is even bad. Not so with Jesus. His words will come forth as instructions of a most amazing nature, possessing a distinguished authority.

Mighty God emerges as a second title for Jesus. Yes, Jesus is God. Beyond being godlike, Jesus will possess all of God's characteristics, including being almighty.

Jesus's third title builds upon his second one: *Everlasting Father*. This is a bit confusing because if Jesus is God's Son, how can he also be the Father? But remember that Jesus and the Father are one. What we see in one, we see in the other. However, let's focus on the word *everlasting*. Jesus is eternal, transcending all time. He participated in creation, and we will celebrate him in the new heaven and new earth, which is to come.

The fourth name for Jesus is *Prince of Peace*. He will usher in an era of perpetual harmony, ruling with excellence for the rest of time.

Last, this child—Jesus, whom God will send— will grow up to rule us. As a descendant of King David, Jesus's government will have no end, for it will extend into eternity. And, unlike human rulers with their frailties, Jesus will oversee his people with perfect, flawless justice.

Jesus is more than our Savior. He is our eternal King, who will usher in peace and rule with perfect justice for all time without end.

Do we stand in astonished awe of who Jesus is and what he has accomplished and will accomplish?

[Discover more about Jesus's characteristics in Luke 4:32, John 1:1–3, John 14:9, John 17:21, Revelation 21:23, and Revelation 22:16.]

Today's reading comes from *Isaiah Bible Study: Discover Jesus, Justice, and Gentiles through the Prophet's Timeless Words.*

DAY 3: CELEBRATE JESUS
LUKE 2:1–20

"I bring you good news that will cause great joy for all the people." (Luke 2:10)

Joseph and his pregnant fiancée travel to Bethlehem for a mandatory census. Unable to find a place to stay, they hunker down in a barn. There, among the filth of livestock, Jesus is born. This is the first Christmas.

Each Christmas my attention focuses on Jesus, the real reason for our annual celebration. In considering the first Christmas, my thoughts are warm and cozy, happy and joyous, idyllic and serene. Angels sing, kings give gifts, and awed shepherds do their shepherding thing.

But all this misses that Jesus is born in someone else's barn, amid unsanitary conditions, and with the stench of animal feces filling the air. It seems so unholy, so unworthy. There's no medical team to monitor Mary's condition or aid in the birth. It's likely just Mary and Joseph trying to figure out what to do. Mary likely helped with the birth of other babies, but I wonder how much Joseph knows about the delivery process. Yet despite all this, Jesus is born.

Once the trauma of delivery passes and the messiness of birth is cleaned up, I envision an awestruck Mary gazing lovingly at this miracle that God produced in her. While nursing him, she strokes his cheek and whispers, "I love you," as only a mother can do.

As Mary overflows with joy and basks in amazement over what God has done, out in the fields a bunch of shepherds are doing their job, unaware of what has happened. Suddenly an angel shows up. He begins by saying what most angels say when they appear before humans, "Don't freak out." Even so, understandably so, the shepherds tremble at his glory. Then the angel says, "Newsflash: A baby has just been born in Bethlehem. He's the Savior. The Messiah you've been longing for." He tells them what to look for: a baby swaddled, abed in a manger.

Then, to underscore the validity of the angel's message, a grand angel choir appears. They chant their praise to God, giving him all glory and blessing the earth with the peace of his favor.

The shepherds rush to Bethlehem to check things out. Just as the angel said, they find the proud parents watching over the baby boy, Jesus, who's sleeping in the animals' feed trough. After confirming what the angel had told them, the shepherds leave and tell everyone they meet about the angel's message and Jesus's birth. Then the shepherds head back to their flocks in awe of God and what he has begun.

The shepherds believe what the angel told them, seek confirmation, and then tell everyone, praising God in the process. They're the world's first missionaries for Jesus. After they leave, Mary grows introspective, pondering and cherishing all these events in her heart.

What do we do with the good news of Jesus? Do we tell others or keep it to ourselves?

[Discover more about Jesus's birth in Matthew 2:1–23.]

Today's reading comes from *Dear Theophilus: A 40-Day Devotional Exploring the Life of Jesus through the Gospel of Luke*.

DAY 4: JOB RESPONDS TO BILDAD
JOB 9–10

"If only there were someone to mediate between us, someone to bring us together, someone to remove God's rod from me, so that his terror would frighten me no more." (Job 9:33–34)

As Bildad sits, a pleased smirk playing on his lips, Job shakes his head and lowers his gaze, fixated on the heap of ashes before him. Bildad's words, too, fell short of the comfort that Job hoped his long-time friend would give. Instead, Bildad's monologue stirred frustration in Job's mind. Without looking up, Job speaks.

"I get what you're saying and agree with it to some extent. But how can I, a mortal man whom God created, prove my innocence to him? He's

God. I'm nobody. He's wise and powerful, controlling his creation with no effort. Who am I to him? I'm nothing. I can't defend myself, debate his decisions, or argue against his wisdom.

"I've done nothing wrong, but he doesn't care. Whether good or bad, we will all die. May my end come soon. If only there were someone to represent me to him, someone who could reconcile us and remove his punishment.

"I hate my life. I plead with the Almighty to give me a not guilty verdict. At least tell me what I've done wrong. As it is, he seems to delight in tormenting me, even though I'm innocent.

"He created me, so I suppose he can do whatever he wants. But does it make sense for him to destroy what he has made? I think not. If only I had died at birth, but here I am. As my life approaches its end, will he relent in his affliction of me—for but a moment—so that I may have one last taste of joy before I die?"

Though Bildad has provided Job with something to think about, it does nothing to ease Job's disquiet. Though Job maintains his innocence, he feels that God has punished him anyway, as though he's guilty. But who is Job to contend with God, to present his case so that he can vindicate himself?

We understand God as approachable. We know he wants us to live in community with him, but Job doesn't see this. Perhaps he can't.

Remember that Job wishes someone could come to mediate between him and God, someone who could bring them together, someone to remove God's punishment and take away Job's fear.

Jesus is that mediator for us. He gave his life for us to reconcile us with Papa, removing our punishment for our wrongdoing and taking away any fear we may have.

Do we see Jesus as our mediator? Have we accepted his work so that we may live in community with him?

[Discover more about Jesus as our mediator and Savior in John 14:6, Romans 8:38–39, Hebrews 9:15, and 1 Timothy 2:5.]

Today's reading comes from *Job Bible Study: Unlock the Drama of Faith, Friends, and Frustration.*

DAY 5: JESUS IS THE WAY
JOHN 14:1–14

Jesus answered, "I am the way and the truth and the life."
(John 14:6)

Jesus has but a few hours left on earth. He wants to make the most of every moment. The teacher gives last-minute instructions to his disciples, trying to encourage them, which they'll need in the days, months, and years ahead. He talks about his father's house with many rooms, about him preparing a place for them, and about him coming back to get them so they can be with him. If this isn't cryptic enough, Jesus adds, "You know the way to where I'm going."

Thomas, one of Jesus's twelve disciples, doesn't. Speaking for the rest of them, he seeks clarification: "We don't know where you're going, so how can we know how to get there?"

Jesus gives him a five-part answer, which John records for us. Jesus says, "I am the way and the truth and the life. No one comes to the Father except through me."

Let's explore this.

First, Jesus opens with, "I am." Don't miss this. In the Old Testament, God the Father tells Moses to think of him as *I am* (Exodus 3:13–14). When Jesus repeats this phrase in his concise answer, it's intentional. We're reminded that Jesus also exists as God, as God the Son. Jesus is the *I am*, just as much as the Father.

Next, Jesus gives the first of three instructive phrases, saying that he is "the way." Jesus himself serves as the path to God the Father. As our Messiah, he points us in the right direction. He provides the means for us to get there. Soon he'll do this by serving as the ultimate sin sacrifice for all of humanity, past, present, and future.

Jesus adds that he is "the truth." He personifies what is real. He exemplifies truth, proclaims truth, and models truth. We can always rely on the words of Jesus as dependable. His words will set us free (John 8:31–32).

After confirming that he is the way and the truth, he adds that he is "the life." Not only does Jesus give us life, but he *is* life. After giving us life at creation, he continues as one who lives forever. We, as his followers, will enjoy eternity with him.

The final of the five key phrases in this verse is "through me." Jesus is the door to Father God. The first four parts of Jesus's answer culminate in his conclusion: through him we reconcile with God the Father, our spiritual Papa.

Jesus supplies what we need for our journey in this life and into the next. He is the source of life, of truth, and of the way to the Father.

Do we trust Jesus to be the way, the truth, and the life? What does this mean to us? How does this influence how we live our life?

[Discover more about Jesus being truth and life in Luke 20:21, John 11:25, and John 18:37.]

Today's reading comes from *Living Water: 40 Reflections on Jesus's Life and Love from the Gospel of John.*

WEEK 2: THE EARTHLY MINISTRY

DAY 6: MINISTRY LAUNCH
MATTHEW 4:12–25

"Come, follow me," Jesus said, "and I will send you out to fish for people." (Matthew 4:19)

Having fasted and withstood Satan's assaults, Jesus is now ready to begin his ministry. He moves from Nazareth to make his home base in Capernaum, around Zebulun and Naphtali. This establishes a fourth location prophesied for Jesus (Isaiah 9:1–2).

In this way, four seemingly contradictory prophecies about the Savior's place of origin all align, producing a unified account.

Jesus begins his ministry with the simple instruction: "Repent." This is because the kingdom of heaven is near (Matthew 4:17). Just as John preached repentance, so, too, does Jesus. Yet the urgency is now greater, for the kingdom of heaven draws near.

As part of his ministry, Jesus picks his first four disciples. Though he could have spread the good news about the kingdom of heaven by himself, he invites others to join him. In this way, he'll prepare them to carry on his ministry once he returns to heaven.

Jesus first taps Peter and his brother Andrew, followed by James and his brother John. They're all fishermen.

When Jesus invites Peter and Andrew to join him, he gives them a most intriguing promise. "Follow me, and you'll fish for people." In doing so, he calls them to a higher purpose. He'll turn their livelihood into a greater vision: fishing for people for Jesus.

How do the brothers respond? They immediately abandon their fishing business and follow Jesus. The brothers don't need to think about it, consult anyone else, or run it by their family. They just leave their work and go all in for Jesus.

What makes this even more remarkable is that we'll later learn that Peter is married. He has a wife to support. How is he to provide for her if he's no longer fishing? He can't. But he answers Jesus's call, making the Messiah a priority for his life. Everything else—even his wife—becomes secondary.

James and John have a similar response. They're in the fishing boat with their dad, preparing their nets to go fishing. When Jesus calls them, they also immediately respond, abandoning their father and the family fishing business.

We applaud them for their commitment to make Jesus first in their lives.

Have we made Jesus first in our lives? What have we given up to follow him?

[Discover more about being a disciple of Jesus in Luke 14:25–35.]

Today's reading comes from *Matthew Bible Study: Discover the Life and Teachings of Jesus.*

DAY 7: JESUS SAVES AND HEALS
MARK 2:1–12

"Which is easier: to say to this paralyzed man, 'Your sins are forgiven,' or to say, 'Get up, take your mat and walk'?"
(Mark 2:9)

Consider that Jesus came to heal and to save. Both aspects of this dual role of his ministry brilliantly emerge in this powerful story of Jesus and the paralyzed man.

After Jesus heals a man of his leprosy, the people come to him from everywhere. He tries to avoid attracting attention to himself (Mark 1:43–45).

A few days later, Jesus teaches inside a house.

The place is packed. Some men bring a paralyzed friend to him, but they can't get inside to reach Jesus. In desperation, they climb onto the roof, make an opening in it, and lower their friend before Jesus.

I wonder why they didn't just wait outside for Jesus to leave and ask him to heal their friend then. It seems like the simpler solution. Yet perhaps they're so focused on getting the help their friend desperately needs that they're not willing to wait. They see an opportunity, and they seize it. I also wonder if they damaged the roof and what the homeowner might have thought about it.

Nevertheless, Jesus finds his teaching interrupted when this paralyzed man descends from the ceiling, suspended in front of him.

Jesus stops his message, for another teachable moment has presented itself.

It's obvious the man is paralyzed, and his pressing need is to walk. Many of the people there likely know this man and his situation.

Mark writes that Jesus sees their faith—the faith of the man's friends. In a surprise move, Jesus confounds everybody by forgiving the man's sins.

Jesus knows this man's greatest need isn't physical but spiritual, so he addresses it first. By offering the man forgiveness, Jesus saves him from his sins. Saving people is one reason Jesus came to earth.

The religious leaders criticize Jesus in their minds. He knows their thoughts and confronts them. He asks them a simple question. "Is it easier to say, 'I forgive your sins' or 'Get up and walk'?"

Anyone can forgive another, but few have God's healing power to restore a paralyzed man.

Knowing it's much easier to say "I forgive your sins" than to make a lame man walk, Jesus heals the man. This addresses the man's second greatest need. In doing so, Jesus proves he also has the power to forgive sins.

In this account, Jesus shows he came not only to save (forgive our sins) but also to heal.

Jesus saves, and Jesus heals.

What do we look to Jesus to do for us? When someone comes to us for help, do we address their biggest need first?

[Discover more about the forgiveness of sins in Psalm 32:1–2, Ephesians 1:7–10, and Colossians 1:13–14.]

Today's reading comes from *Mark Bible Study: Discover the Transformative Truths of Jesus.*

DAY 8: FULFILL THE LAW
MATTHEW 5

"Do not think that I have come to abolish the Law or the Prophets; I have not come to abolish them but to fulfill them."
(Matthew 5:17)

When many people read this verse, they focus on the word *fulfill*. They assume that once Jesus fulfills the Law and the Prophets, those rules no longer apply. They think they can disregard what the Old Testament says.

This, however, is a wrong interpretation. Jesus says so. Our Savior states unequivocally that he is not abolishing the teachings of the Law and the

Prophets. He isn't replacing them nor negating them. They still apply.

In this way, we can better understand the use of the word *fulfill* to mean *extend* or *expand*. Jesus's purpose in showing us a new way to the Father is to extend the Old Testament Law and Prophets. This means they still apply to us today, but in a new, expanded way.

As Jesus continues his sermon, he shares examples of how he fulfills the Law and the Prophets.

First up is **murder**. We know murder is wrong. The Law says so, and we follow that today. Yet Jesus extends the concept. If we become angry at another, we are just as guilty.

Next, we read about **adultery**. We likewise know adultery is wrong. We see that in the Old Testament and continue to affirm it. Jesus also extends what this means. He says that if we look at another person with lust, we've already committed adultery in our hearts. From Jesus's perspective, this is just as bad as doing it with our bodies.

Then Jesus moves on to **divorce**. The Law made it easy for a man to divorce his wife. At least that's what the people in Jesus's day thought. But Jesus sets a higher standard. He clarifies that the only justification for divorce is unfaithfulness. Aside from that, he expects people to honor their marriage vows.

Fourth, Jesus talks about **revenge**. Moses stated, "an eye for an eye and a tooth for a tooth." This kept people from overreacting with excessive retaliation when wronged. A Biblical example occurs when Dinah's brothers slaughter all the men in the town because one of them raped her (Genesis 34). Lest we think too harshly of her brothers' actions, remember that they lived prior to Moses giving the people this instruction.

But Jesus goes beyond the concept of limiting our retaliation to a reciprocal response. He tells us not to take revenge at all, even to the point of doing more than requested.

The fifth example is about how we treat others. The Old Testament says we are to **love our neighbors** as much as we love ourselves. Some might infer that this gives us permission to hate our enemies. The people in the Old Testament thought so. Again, Jesus extends the concept of loving our neighbors into a command to pray for our enemies.

These show us five ways Jesus fulfills the Law and the Prophets. From this we can learn that when we encounter an Old Testament command, we shouldn't be quick to dismiss it. Instead, we should consider how Jesus wants us to fulfill that command today.

What parts of the Law have we dismissed as irrelevant? What Old Testament commands can we extend to apply to us today?

[Discover more about these five commands in Exodus 20:13, Exodus 20:14, Exodus 21:23–25, Deuteronomy 24:1, and Leviticus 19:18.]

Today's reading comes from *Matthew Bible Study: Discover the Life and Teachings of Jesus.*

DAY 9: ASK GOD FOR WISDOM
JAMES 1:5–8

If any of you lacks wisdom, you should ask God, who gives generously to all without finding fault, and it will be given to you. (James 1:5)

Another popular verse in the letter of James comes next. It's a personal favorite. James states that if we lack wisdom, we should ask God.

He's generous, without restrictions. He will give us wisdom. It's that simple.

There is, however, a caveat. When we ask for wisdom, we must believe that God will provide and not doubt. Doubt causes uncertainty, which James equates to an ocean wave tossing about. If we doubt, we shouldn't expect to receive anything from God, including wisdom. A person who doubts is double-minded. Their uncertainty offsets their confidence in receiving what they requested.

Suddenly the simple prayer of asking for wisdom and receiving it doesn't seem so easy.

Obviously, it's best to pray full of faith and without an ounce of doubt. Yet this doesn't mean that doubt automatically negates the effectiveness of our prayers.

Consider Peter. His faith in Jesus's command to come to him allows the disciple to walk on water. But when he takes his eyes off Jesus and looks at the physical environment around him, he doubts. He sinks. Yet Jesus rescues him, despite his doubt (Matthew 14:29–31).

Peter started his trip walking on water full of faith. He believed that through Jesus he could do the impossible. And he did—for a while. Yet, despite his initial success, doubt assaulted him and caused him to question what he was doing. That's when he faltered. But Jesus was there for him when he did. Jesus's reaction to Peter's uncertainty can comfort us when we struggle to fully believe.

Before we criticize Peter too heavily for his understandable doubt, remember that he was the only disciple with enough faith to get out of the boat. Instead of chastising him for a moment of doubt, we should celebrate him for his faith to act.

Another time, a father comes to Jesus. He asks the healer to drive out an evil spirit from his boy. The disciples had already tried and failed, so the dad may wonder whether Jesus can. The man conditions his request for healing with the tentative word *if.*

Jesus seems a bit insulted. He says anything is possible if we believe.

The man gives a most honest—and insightful—response. He says, "I do believe! Help me overcome my unbelief." Then Jesus heals the boy (Mark 9:17–27).

This story should provide us with much comfort when in the presence of doubt. This father had an element of belief paired with nonbelief. The two coexisted as a jumbled conflict in his mind. Yet he implicitly turned his doubts over to Jesus. And that was it.

We can learn from this example when we ask God for wisdom. We ask in faith, and we ask him to take away our doubts. When we do, we can expect to receive wisdom, just as the man received healing for his son.

What is our reaction to doubt? Have we asked Jesus to take our doubts away?

[Discover more about wisdom in James 3:13–17.]

Today's reading comes from *James & Jude Bible Study: Discover 40 Practical Insights from Jesus's Brothers.*

DAY 10: CONFESS OUR SINS
1 JOHN 1:8–10

If we confess our sins, he is faithful and just and will forgive us our sins and purify us from all unrighteousness. (1 John 1:9)

As a young teen, I had a Sunday school teacher who claimed he sometimes would go an entire day without sinning. Granted, he didn't claim to be without sin, only that he had some days where he avoided it.

Though he was a godly man and I respected him deeply, I questioned if such a thing were possible. At least I doubted it was for me. It could be I was too sensitive to sin or wrongly confused temptation with sin, but I wondered if I could even go one hour without sinning, let alone twenty-four.

Today's trio of verses addresses sin and our attitude toward it. This passage opens and closes with parallel verses that restate the same idea: if we claim to live a life without sin, we delude ourselves. (My teacher only claimed to be sinless for a day, not a lifetime.)

Scripture says that everyone has sinned and falls short of God's expectations (Romans 3:23). Therefore, if we claim we're sinless, we make God out to be a liar and do not accept his truth.

Fortunately, we don't need to wallow in our sinfulness. Sandwiched between these two verses about our sin-filled nature, we find a most encouraging promise.

John says if we confess our sins, God will forgive them, purifying us from our unrighteousness, that is, from our wrong behavior. We can count on it.

John also writes that Jesus died for the sins of the entire world (1 John 2:2), but we don't automatically receive his forgiveness. Through this sacrificial death, Jesus has prepared the gift of salvation for everyone. But until we receive his present it's not ours.

We can receive Jesus's gift of salvation when we

admit our faults. But to do that, we must first acknowledge that our sins need forgiving.

When we confess our sins, that is, admit our faults to Jesus, we can have confidence in his response of forgiveness. This is because he's already died for our sins to make us right with Father God. He will be faithful to forgive. And his forgiveness is because his death satisfied what justice demands. This is what it means when John writes that Jesus is faithful and just.

When we confess our sins, we will receive his forgiveness. This purifies us from all the wrongs we have done and all the wrong things we will do.

Have we confessed our sins to Jesus and received his forgiveness? How should we live our life knowing that he has purified us from our unrighteousness?

[Discover more about confession in Psalm 32:5, Proverbs 28:13, and Acts 19:18.]

Today's reading comes from *1, 2, & 3 John Bible*

Study: Unpacking the Simple Yet Profound Truths of John's Epistles.

WEEK 3: THE RADICAL CALL OF DISCIPLESHIP

DAY 11: BE LIKE JESUS
1 JOHN 2:3–6

Whoever claims to live in him must live as Jesus did.
(1 John 2:6)

Today's passage talks about knowing God and keeping his commands. If we claim to know God and don't do what he says, we're only deluding ourselves from the truth, and our claim is false. But when we obey his commands our love for God is complete.

In short, as his followers, we must live as he lived. We must be like Jesus.

We are fortunate to have four biographies of Jesus in the Bible to inform us about how he lived. They are the books of Matthew, Mark, Luke, and

John. By reading them we know what Jesus does during his time here on earth. Then we can follow his example and be more like him.

We don't have to follow a bunch of rules with legalistic fervor or adhere to an extensive list of ritualistic commands like we find in the Old Testament. We must simply be like Jesus. It's that easy.

Here are some of the things that Jesus does:

- Jesus makes his relationship with his Father a priority. From an early age, Jesus puts his Father in heaven first (Luke 2:49). This is what matters most.
- Jesus takes care of himself so that he can take care of his followers. Jesus knows that if he isn't spiritually healthy, he can't expect to be at his best to help others (Matthew 14:23).
- Jesus has time for everyone who comes to him. While going to heal Jairus's daughter, he pauses to heal a sick woman (Luke 8:40–56). He stays in Samaria for two extra days simply because the people ask him to (John 4:40).

- Jesus teaches others about God. Jesus speaks with authority and not like other religious leaders (Mark 1:22). He instructs people using parables (Mark 4:2). His longest message in the Bible is the Sermon on the Mount (Matthew 5–7).
- Jesus heals others (Matthew 8:14–15). And he says his followers will do the same (John 14:12).
- Jesus opposes religious hypocrisy (Luke 13:15).
- Jesus offers love to everyone (Mark 10:21 and John 11:3–5).
- Jesus forgives and doesn't judge (John 8:3–11).
- Jesus is never in a hurry (John 11:6).
- Jesus models right behavior for his disciples and followers (John 13:15).

By following these examples of Jesus, we can live as Jesus models for us and know that we are in him.

What can we do to be more like Jesus? What must we stop doing?

[Discover more about being an example in 1 Corinthians 11:1 and 1 Peter 2:21.]

Today's reading comes from *1, 2, & 3 John Bible Study: Unpacking the Simple Yet Profound Truths of John's Epistles.*

DAY 12: LEAVE IT ALL BEHIND
MARK 10:1–31

Then Peter spoke up, "We have left everything to follow you!"
(Mark 10:28)

A rich man runs up to Jesus and kneels before the Teacher. He asks a simple question: "What must I do to receive eternal life?"

Jesus refers him to some of the key commandments: do not murder, do not commit adultery, do not steal, and do not give false testimony. Another is to honor your father and mother. These are five of the Ten Commandments as found in the law of Moses (Exodus 20:12–16 and Deuteronomy 5:16–20).

Jesus's answer encourages the man.

"I've done all these things since I was a kid," the man says. He must have a smug satisfaction. He surely thinks he's in, that Jesus will affirm his right living as enough to qualify him to receive eternal life.

Not so.

Jesus looks at the man in love and tells him to do one more thing. "Give everything you have to the poor. Then come and follow me."

The man's expectations fall. He slinks away in sadness because he is very wealthy.

Then Jesus tells his disciples, "It's hard for rich people to enter the kingdom of God."

This shocks the disciples. They assumed righteous living would qualify them. They assumed rich people had an edge and received favor in their standing with God. Now they know that right living isn't enough to earn salvation, and money can't buy eternal life.

"How then can anyone be saved?" they ask.

"With men, it's impossible," Jesus states unequivocally. "But with God, all things are possible."

As expected, Peter reacts first. "We left everything to follow you."

Jesus lists things people may give up when they follow him. This includes their home, family, and possessions. Jesus promises they'll receive a hundredfold return in this world. Then they'll receive eternal life when they die.

Jesus's promise of a hundredfold return for what we give up when we follow him and share his good news may seem like hyperbole—an unrealistic outcome. Yet we might be better off to not think in physical terms but in spiritual.

Recall the parable of the sower where a good seed produces a hundredfold return. As we invite people to follow Jesus, we might get a hundredfold return for the seeds we plant. Spiritually, they become our home, our family, and even our possessions. This is our reward in this world. Then we'll spend eternity with them in the next. This is even better,

Giving everything to Jesus and following him is what matters.

What are we trying to do to earn—or maintain—our salvation? What are we holding onto that keeps us from truly following Jesus?

[Discover more about putting the past behind us in Genesis 19:26 and Luke 9:62. Read Jesus's definition of family in Mark 3:33–34.]

54

Today's reading comes from *Mark Bible Study: Discover the Transformative Truths of Jesus.*

DAY 13: LOVE YOUR NEIGHBOR
LUKE 10:25–37

"'Love the Lord your God with all your heart and with all your soul and with all your strength and with all your mind'; and, 'Love your neighbor as yourself.'" (Luke 10:27)

We call one of Jesus's more beloved teachings the Parable of the Good Samaritan. While the name for this parable comes from its main character, a better name is the Parable of Loving Your Neighbor.

Our story starts, like many of them do, with someone coming to Jesus to test him. The person is an expert in the law. Today we might call him a theologian. Let that sink in.

This person doesn't have a genuine question for

Jesus. Instead he seeks to make Jesus look bad and himself look good. Despite this, he poses a good question. He asks, "What must I do to receive life eternal?" Who doesn't want to know the answer to that?

As is often the case, Jesus responds to the question with another question. He asks the man, "What does the Law of Moses say about it?"

The theologian is ready with an answer. He says, "Love God totally, and then love your neighbor as much as you care for yourself."

"Correct," Jesus says. These two actions smartly summarize the Law of Moses. "Now, go do this and live."

The theologian squirms. He knows he falls short. He seeks a way out, a loophole to justify his unloving behavior. "Well," he says, "who is my neighbor, anyway?"

Jesus responds with his famous parable of The Good Samaritan. Here's a condensed version: a man gets beat up, robbed, and left to die. A priest—a religious VIP—walks by but doesn't check on the injured guy. A Levite—another religious person—passes by and doesn't help either. A Samaritan—a race despised by most Jews—sees the man and has compassion on him. At risk of also being robbed and beaten, the Samaritan invests his time and money to care for the injured man and make sure he'll be all right.

Then Jesus asks the theologian, "Which of these three men was a good neighbor?"

Unwilling to say "Samaritan" out loud, the theologian merely mumbles, "The one who showed mercy."

Jesus says, "Go and do the same."

The theologian must be in dismay. His plan backfired, and he's embarrassed.

Here are the key points.

First, Jesus confirms the way to eternal life is to love God and love our neighbors.

Second, the definition of neighbor is quite broad. It means everyone.

Third, the star of the story, the one with the right behavior, comes from a race the Jews look down on. He's an outsider, an outcast. The hero is a nobody. This should encourage everyone who doesn't fit in with religious institutions' or society's expectations. That means me, and it may mean you.

Is loving God and loving our neighbors enough to be right with God? How can we love our neighbors as God intends?

[Discover more about love in Leviticus 19:18, Deuteronomy 6:5, and 1 John 4:7–8.]

Today's reading comes from *Dear Theophilus: A 40-Day Devotional Exploring the Life of Jesus through the Gospel of Luke.*

DAY 14: LOVE ONE ANOTHER
1 JOHN 3:11–15

For this is the message you heard from the beginning: We should love one another. (1 John 3:11)

John tells his audience that we are to love one another.

It's not a new command but one we've heard from the beginning. He first mentions this in 1 John 2:7–8. And now he tells us what this command is: we are to love one another. It's that simple.

Saying that we've heard this from "the beginning" centers on Jesus.

When an expert in the law asks Jesus to name the greatest command, he says it's to love God.

Then he tacks on a second one—which makes it the second greatest command—to love others. In a most effective manner, these summarize everything in the Old Testament (Matthew 22:35–40).

We are to love God and love one another.

Jesus also talks about the importance of loving one another in his Sermon on the Mount. In that message he tells his listeners to love others in the same way that they love themselves (Matthew 7:12). He says the same thing, although more succinctly, in his Sermon on the Plain (Luke 6:31).

Though it's through Jesus that we get this essential command to love one another, we find it throughout the Old Testament. All the commands God gives his people either relate to their relationship with him or their relationship with others. As we've already mentioned, this comes from the Ten Commandments too. We first love God (commandments one through four) and then we love others (commandments five through ten).

This is why Jesus says the greatest command is to love God and the second greatest is to love others. Everything else in the Old Testament underscores these two (Matthew 22:37–40).

We find this command to love others hidden in the Levitical law too. Quoting the words of Father

God, Moses writes that we are to love our neighbors in the same way we love ourselves (Leviticus 19:18), which Jesus later quotes in Matthew 22:39.

Paul reiterates this in his letter to the church in Rome. He says we should owe no outstanding debt other than the continuing debt to love one another. When we do this, we fulfill the Old Testament commands (Romans 13:8).

In his letter to the church in Galatia, Paul confirms that we can keep the entire law by obeying the singular command to love our neighbor as much as we love ourselves (Galatians 5:14).

This command to love one another as we love ourselves is the essence of the Golden Rule. We are to treat others the way we want them to treat us. This means doing for them the same things that we'd like to receive ourselves. It also means not doing to them the things we don't want to receive. The Golden Rule is based on the Bible, going back to Leviticus 19:18.

This idea of loving one another as we love ourselves permeates Scripture. It's been there since the beginning.

What must we do differently to more fully obey God's essential command to love our neighbor? Beyond that, how well do we obey God's greatest command to love him?

[Discover more about John's instructions to love one another in John 13:34, John 13:35, 1 John 3:11, 1 John 3:23, 1 John 4:7, 1 John 4:11, 1 John 4:12, and 2 John 1:5.]

Today's reading comes from *1, 2, & 3 John Bible Study: Unpacking the Simple Yet Profound Truths of John's Epistles.*

DAY 15: COUNT THE COST
OF FOLLOWING JESUS

LUKE 14:25–35

"If anyone comes to me and does not hate father and mother, wife and children, brothers and sisters—yes, even their own life—such a person cannot be my disciple." (Luke 14:26)

On one of Jesus's travels, a large crowd trails behind him. He turns to them to talk about what it takes to truly follow him and be his disciple.

In doing so, Jesus uses some strong language. He uses the word hate.

He says that if we want to be his disciple—a true disciple—we must hate our parents, our spouse, our children, and our siblings. We must even hate our own life. Then he says we should pick up our cross and follow him.

What does he mean about picking up our cross? He's building upon his prior thought about hating our own life. In his day, prisoners dragged their cross through the city on their way to the execution site. For his followers to do this would confirm their allegiance to him and their willingness to die. That's commitment.

These are some serious barriers to deal with. Does Jesus really want us to hate our family and despise our own life to the point of death before we can fully follow him?

No.

Jesus uses exaggeration to make his point. He wants disciples who will make him their priority. He wants disciples to consider what it will cost to follow him. They must commit fully.

He shares two short parables to explain.

The first is a builder who wants to erect a tower. Before he starts, he figures out the total cost of the project. This will save him embarrassment from starting construction and not having enough money to finish. So, too, when we decide to follow Jesus.

The second is a king about to go into battle. Won't he first analyze the situation and look at troop strength to see if he can hope to defeat his enemy? And if he doesn't expect to win, wouldn't he pursue a peaceful solution instead of fighting?

Jesus doesn't want us to say we'll follow him and be his disciples if we don't really mean it, if we haven't considered what it will take to go all in for him. He's not trying to talk us out of it, but he wants us to contemplate what it may cost us to put him first in our lives. First over everything else.

Though we may say we put Jesus first, do our actions confirm it?

[Discover more about following Jesus in Luke 9:23 and Luke 9:57–62.]

Today's reading comes from *Dear Theophilus: A 40-Day Devotional Exploring the Life of Jesus through the Gospel of Luke.*

WEEK 4: THE ULTIMATE SACRIFICE

DAY 16: PROPHECY FULFILLED
ZECHARIAH 9–10

*See, your king comes to you, righteous and victorious, lowly
and riding on a donkey, on a colt, the foal of a donkey.*
(Zechariah 9:9)

Babylon has conquered God's chosen people, deporting many of them. Those who remain in Jerusalem and throughout what's left of the nation of Judah struggle to eke out their survival. They're broken, abased, and vulnerable. They so need the Savior—whom the prophets foretold—to rescue them. So when Zechariah prophesies their King coming to them, they see this as reinforcing past prophecies. Their Savior will emerge as an answer to their prayers and the fulfillment of many predictions.

But their King doesn't come charging in on a stallion, armed for battle, and leading a mighty military force. He comes in humility, riding a donkey. This is a sign of peace. He comes in peace, and he will promote peace.

Though the people long for a physical savior, God will send them a spiritual Savior—which is far better.

Let's fast-forward to the New Testament and read about the fulfillment of Zechariah's prophecy. Matthew, Mark, and John all record this event in their biographies of Jesus. It happens on what we call Palm Sunday, a few days before Jesus's execution (Good Friday) and subsequent resurrection (Easter).

Here's what happens. As Jesus and his team walk toward Jerusalem, he sends two from his group to go on ahead to the village and look for a colt. They'll find the animal tied there, one that no one has ever ridden. They're to unfasten him and bring him to Jesus. If anyone asks what they're doing, they are to say, "The Lord needs to borrow him and will return him in a bit."

The pair do as Jesus instructed. And just as he

said, they find the colt. When they untie him, some people question them, assuming they're thieves. But once the two disciples give Jesus's answer, the people let them go.

The pair bring the colt to Jesus and throw their coats onto the animal's back to provide a makeshift saddle. Jesus mounts the colt—remember, no one's ever ridden him before, so the animal's nature is to fight anyone who climbs on his back, but this doesn't happen. Jesus rides the animal into Jerusalem. And as he does, the people line the path, spreading their coats and palm branches out before him. They shout their praise to the Lord, acknowledging Jesus as their King. Lest we have any doubt, Matthew and John both note that this fulfills Zechariah's prediction.

This is just one of the awesome ways that Jesus accomplishes Old Testament prophecy.

Do we celebrate Jesus the way the people did on the first Palm Sunday? Are we in awe of how he fulfills what the prophets foretold?

[Discover more about the fulfillment of Zechariah's prophecy in Matthew 21:1–11, Mark 11:1–11, and John 12:12–19.]

72

Today's reading comes from *Minor Prophets Bible Study: Unearth Timeless Teachings of the Bible's Unsung Prophets.*

DAY 17: THE LORD'S SUPPER
MARK 14:1–26

"This is my blood of the covenant, which is poured out for many." (Mark 14:24)

Jesus continues to move toward his sacrificial death on our behalf; it is but days away. A woman anoints his head with expensive oil, which Jesus proclaims as a beautiful act that prepares his body for burial. I'm sure none of the people knew what he was talking about then, but we certainly do now.

Two days later, Jesus sends a pair of disciples into the city to prepare for their Passover celebration. He gives them some cryptic instructions.

Once in the city, they're to look for a man carrying a jar of water. They should follow him. When he reaches his destination, they're to say to the owner of the house, "The Teacher wants to know where the guestroom is so he can eat Passover with his disciples." The man will take them to a room furnished and ready. That's where they're to prepare the Passover meal.

Moses instituted Passover as a family celebration done at home, but Jesus's family isn't there. They're back where he grew up. So are his disciples' families. Yet, as Jesus already said, those who do God's will are his family (Mark 3:34–35). This includes his disciples. In the absence of his biological family, it's fitting that Jesus will spend Passover with his spiritual family and they with him.

The headings added to some Bibles for this passage call it "The Last Supper." Although it will in fact be Jesus's last supper before his arrest, it's the first supper for those of us who follow him.

Today this meal goes by various names—the Lord's Supper, Holy Communion, and the Eucharist—even though these last two labels aren't found in the Bible. Regardless of what we call it, it's when Jesus takes the tradition of the Passover meal and turns it into a celebration of his sacrificial death.

Passover remembers God delivering the people from their physical bondage to slavery, while Communion remembers Jesus delivering us from our spiritual bondage to sin.

As they eat their meal, Jesus takes a loaf of bread. He thanks Papa for it. He breaks it and gives it to his disciples to eat. Then he says, "This is my body."

Next Jesus takes a cup and gives thanks for it too. He gives it to them, and they drink. He says, "My blood is a new covenant, poured out for many."

Then they sing a song and walk to the Mount of Olives. Though the disciples don't know what's about to happen, Jesus does. So do we.

We should remember this each time we take Communion.

What does Communion mean to us today? How can we better align our practice of the Lord's Supper with what Jesus implemented and the Passover celebration it's based on?

[Discover more about this solemn celebration in 1 Corinthians 11:23–26.]

Today's reading comes from *Mark Bible Study: Discover the Transformative Truths of Jesus.*

DAY 18: THE FINAL SACRIFICE
HEBREWS 9:16–28

Christ was sacrificed once to take away the sins of many; and he will appear a second time, not to bear sin, but to bring salvation. (Hebrews 9:28)

We're not wrong to consider a covenant like a will. A will doesn't go into effect until after death occurs. Under the old covenant this was the death of an animal. Under Jesus's new covenant it is *his* death. In both cases, death sets in motion what each covenant specifies.

As the old covenant requires the spilling of blood, so too does the new one. Though the old covenant demands an annual blood sacrifice of animals, the new covenant does not. As the perfect human sacrifice, Jesus's death ends the need for ongoing animal sacrifices that only temporarily cleanse the people of their sins.

The writers of Hebrews remind us that Jesus doesn't enter the earthly replica of the tabernacle when he dies. Instead, he enters heaven itself, into God's very presence. In addition, Jesus doesn't need to do this over and over, as did the high priests under the old covenant. Jesus suffers and dies one time. Once is enough. Jesus's death is the final sacrifice to remove the sins of all people throughout all time.

In this way Jesus comes to earth to die once, removing the sins of many. And he will appear a second time, not to die again, but to bring salvation to those who await him with expectation.

We can interpret this second appearance of Jesus in multiple ways. Here are two thoughts.

Just as he ascended into heaven after he rose from the dead, he will one day descend from heaven and return to earth (Acts 1:10–11). Then he will gather his followers and take them to be with him forever (John 14:2–3).

This will complete his saving work. This promise, however, doesn't apply to every believer but only to those living when he returns. Those who died prior to his second coming will already be with him.

Another understanding of his second appearance is to compare this with the high priests' annual duty under the old covenant. The people see the high priest enter the Most Holy Place to offer the annual sacrifice. But they can't see what he's doing. They don't know when he finishes.

Instead, they wait outside for the high priest to emerge from the Most Holy Place. Only when they see him a second time do they know the sacrifice has been completed. Then they can have assurance their sins are covered—for one more year.

In the same way as these Old Testament high priests, Jesus appears the second time to confirm the sacrifice has been completed. His death represents the final sacrifice, the sacrifice to end them all.

Though this second explanation may not mean much to us today, the Hebrew people of old—the recipients of the letter to the Hebrews—would have certainly grasped the connection. It would comfort them, tying the old covenant that they know well with Jesus's new covenant that they're just beginning to embrace.

Are we awaiting Jesus's return with eager expectation? What will he find us doing when he returns a second time?

[Discover a parallel story about another priest serving in the temple—offering the daily burning of incense—in Luke 1:8–22.]

Today's reading comes from *Hebrews Bible Study: A 40-Day Exploration of Faith, Perseverance, and Godly Living.*

DAY 19: ALIVE IN THE SPIRIT
1 PETER 3:18–19

For Christ also suffered once for sins, the righteous for the unrighteous, to bring you to God. He was put to death in the body but made alive in the Spirit. (1 Peter 3:18)

Today's passage is one of the most concise and yet richest explanations in the Bible about salvation through Jesus. We will do well to study it, internalize it, and use it to shape our understanding of who Jesus is and what he did for us.

This verse—and our salvation—starts with Christ, which means Messiah. Jesus is the Messiah. That is, Jesus is the Christ, which people often shorten to Jesus Christ or sometimes simply Christ.

Without Christ as our Messiah, we couldn't receive our salvation. It all hinges on him and not ourselves. We only need to receive—through faith—what he did for us (Romans 10:10 and Hebrews 10:39).

Jesus suffered once—and only once—for all our sins. This is unlike the Old Testament sacrifices, which repeated annually to atone for the sins the people committed that year. Then they had to do it again the next year: year after year, over and over.

Jesus's sacrifice is a once-for-all ransom of us. In his singular sacrifice—during which he received and carried the punishment for all our wrongs—he died for all the sins, of all people, through all time. He died to cover our past mistakes and our future blunders, the ones we haven't yet made. Besides our own sins, he died for all the sins of those who've gone before us and for all the sins of those who will follow us.

Jesus is sinless. He is righteous. We are not. We are sinful. On our own, we are unrighteous. Yet the righteous Jesus died for his unrighteous creation. The righteous for the unrighteous. The sinless for the sinner. Jesus for us—for you and for me.

In dying for us, Jesus does so to bring us to Father God through him. In this way, we are reconciled to Papa. Jesus is the only way to the Father (John 14:6). There are no other paths to salvation.

When Jesus died on the cross as the ultimate sacrifice to end all sacrifices, his body suffered death, but this wasn't the end. Even though the physical part of him died, the spiritual part of him did not. His physical death makes him spiritually alive—again.

He becomes spiritually alive just as he was before he came to earth as a baby to save us, and just as he is today waiting for us to join him when our physical bodies die (John 14:1–3). Then we, too, will be alive in the Spirit.

What part of this verse do we appreciate the most? How can we best thank Jesus for saving us?

[Discover more about salvation in Ephesians 2:8–9.]

Today's reading comes from *1 & 2 Peter Bible Study: Practical Teaching and Profound Insights from Peter's Letters to Jesus's Church.*

DAY 20: A NEW COVENANT
HEBREWS 8:1–6

The ministry Jesus has received is as superior to theirs as the covenant of which he is mediator is superior to the old one.
(Hebrews 8:6)

Hebrews 7 explains about the need for a new priesthood to replace the old one, one which the Hebrew people are most familiar with. Lest there be any doubt, Jesus is this new high priest. But unlike all those high priests who descended from Aaron and preceded him Jesus as our high priest is unique.

After his resurrection from the dead, Jesus ascends into heaven. He sits at the right hand of the

Father's throne. There, Jesus serves in the heavenly sanctuary—the true tabernacle. God himself established this supernatural temple, one far superior to the one built on earth by human hands.

This tabernacle here on earth, along with the temple that replaced it, serves as mere copies of the original one in heaven, a shadow of what exists in the supernatural realm. Though the heavenly version far exceeds its earthly counterpart, the two parallel each other, with the earthly one revealing truth to us about the heavenly one.

We get a sense of the importance of their similarity because God warned Moses to build the tabernacle exactly how the Almighty had instructed his servant (Exodus 25:40). This occurred when Moses went up Mount Sinai and spent forty days with God to receive detailed instructions about the tabernacle, worship, and right living (Exodus 24–31).

If it's critical for the construction of the tabernacle on earth to match what is in heaven, there must be a reason for it.

I sense the earthly tabernacle/temple is connected to the supernatural one in heaven, linking the two together. When Jesus dies and the veil in the temple tears in half here on earth, I envision the corresponding veil in the heavenly counterpart simultaneously rending. On earth this symbolically shows we have direct access to God in the Most Holy Place, whereas in heaven our access is tangible to the very throne of God and his presence. This, of course, is merely how I envision it.

Returning to today's text, this discussion about the earthly tabernacle mimicking the superior one in heaven, shows that Jesus's ministry is in the same way superior to the priesthood of the Old Testament. It also shows us that the new covenant through Jesus, which he mediates, is likewise superior to the old one.

This is because the new covenant offers us better promises. It pledges to give us the forgiveness of sin and life eternal with God in heaven.

In what other ways might it be important for the earthly tabernacle to match the model in heaven? How is Jesus's ministry superior to that of the Old Testament high priests?

[Discover more about the tabernacle in Acts 7:44–50 and Revelation 15:5.]

Today's reading comes from *Hebrews Bible Study: A 40-Day Exploration of Faith, Perseverance, and Godly Living.*

WEEK 5: THE RISEN LORD AND HIS SPIRIT

DAY 21: WE ARE ON
THE WINNING SIDE

JOHN 16:16–33

"Take heart! I have overcome the world." (John 16:33)

As Jesus continues his last instructions to his disciples, he talks of his departure, which his disciples will mourn, and the world will celebrate. But as a woman struggles through childbirth, and then rejoices over the birth of her baby, so too the disciples' grief will turn into joy. Jesus will see them again, which means they'll see him again. No one will be able to steal their joy in Jesus. He continues to offer encouragement, mentioning answered prayer and Father God's love for them.

The disciples start to understand. At last, they

believe. This is a good thing because he has little time left to explain, so they better understand now.

He affirms their belief in him and warns they'll soon scatter, each retreating to his own home. Though they will leave him, Jesus won't be alone. His Father will stay.

Jesus says he's telling them these things to give them peace. And even though the world will pile trouble upon them, "Don't worry," Jesus says, "I have overcome the world."

Jesus wants them not to worry but to overflow with peace. By extension, he tells us the same.

Worry occurs when we look at our life from a human perspective. We see threats all around us, we feel the burden of living for Jesus in a world that is against him, and we combat an enemy set on causing us pain. These worries can weigh us down and rob us of our peace.

Yet, through God's perspective, we can see through fresh eyes. We know how the story ends. We know that Jesus, through his ultimate sacrifice, has forgiven our sins and defeated the evil one. He has overcome. Though we may not realize the full release that his victory gives us now, we will experience it completely as we persist in following him and being his disciple. This should fill us with peace.

Since Jesus has overcome the world, if we believe in him and follow him, we, too, can overcome our world through him. If we align with Jesus, we are on the winning side.

Are we winning through Jesus? How does knowing that Jesus overcame the world guide our attitudes and actions?

[Discover what else John says about overcoming the world and the evil one in 1 John 2:13–14, 4:4, and 5:1–5.]

Today's reading comes from *Living Water: 40 Reflections on Jesus's Life and Love from the Gospel of John.*

DAY 22: GO
MATTHEW 28

"Therefore go and make disciples of all nations, baptizing them in the name of the Father and of the Son and of the Holy Spirit, and teaching them to obey everything I have commanded you." (Matthew 28:19–20)

The story of Jesus's sacrifice to make us right with Father God doesn't end with his death. Nor does it end with his burial. Instead, his story continues. A few days later, Jesus rises from the grave. He overcomes death, proving his mastery over it.

Yet he doesn't intend to stay on earth in his resurrected form to lead his disciples. Instead, he will return to heaven and send them the Holy

Spirit. It's the Holy Spirit who will lead his disciples to grow Jesus's following.

Before the Savior returns to heaven, however, he gives his followers his final instructions. Matthew concludes his biography of Jesus with this as his last teaching to his followers.

We often call this the Great Commission. In this, he commissions his disciples for ministry, the greatest ministry they could ever pursue.

He tells them to go and make disciples. It's that simple. Where are they to go? It's not a message just for the Jews, God's chosen people. Instead, they're to go to all nations. That's everywhere and includes everyone. Salvation isn't just for the Jews. It's for the Gentiles as well. This means it's for you and me too.

As the disciples go and make disciples, there are two parts to their mission.

First, they need to baptize people in the name of the Father, Son, and Holy Spirit. Baptism is a public display of the people's commitment to follow Jesus. It extends the Old Testament ceremonial washing to make the priests clean. Though baptism doesn't actually wash our sins away, it shows we're clean through Jesus.

Symbolically, baptism—going into the water and emerging from it—gives us a visual reminder of

Jesus's death, burial, and resurrection. It's a beautiful rite.

The second part of making disciples is to teach the people everything about Jesus and to obey his instructions. We know what Jesus taught and commanded through Matthew's record of his life, along with the books of Mark, Luke, and John. Through these accounts, we can learn about Jesus and what he told us to do.

Then we must obey everything he said.

What can we do to go and make disciples? As we teach others to obey Jesus's commands, how can we better serve as an example?

[Discover more about Jesus's last instructions in Mark 16:15–18 and Acts 1:4–9.]

Today's reading comes from *Matthew Bible Study: Discover the Life and Teachings of Jesus.*

DAY 23: WAIT FOR IT
ACTS 1:1–8

"Do not leave Jerusalem, but wait for the gift my Father promised, which you have heard me speak about." (Acts 1:4)

Acts picks up where the book of Luke ended. As with many sequels, Acts opens with a review of what happened in the first book. Again addressing Theophilus, Luke references his first letter, which we call Luke, the third book in the New Testament.

Here's the recap: In the forty days between Jesus's resurrection and his return to heaven, he appears to his followers many times. He proves he's alive and reminds them about the kingdom of God. Slowly, things begin to click for them. Jesus isn't a military leader who will overthrow the Roman rule. He's a spiritual revolutionary to fulfill God's plan for humanity, set in motion before time began.

Finally, Jesus's teaching starts to take on new meaning. The misconceptions of his followers' prior thinking fall away. But it takes time to reorient their perspective from the physical world to a spiritual reality. When one of his followers asks if Jesus is ready to restore Israel as a nation, his answer is "not now." The timing is secret.

Instead, Jesus tells his followers to wait.

Waiting is counter to our modern-day thinking. Delay represents lost opportunity. We must maintain momentum to propel our cause forward. Yet Jesus says, "Wait." It seems ill-advised. However, much of what Jesus says is contrary to human wisdom. We should expect the unexpected from Jesus. If he says to wait, this shouldn't cause dismay. Sometimes inaction is the best action—especially when God says to delay.

From a human perspective, they should organize, plan, and deploy across the region to tell others about Jesus. They have experience going out two-by-two. Jesus trained them to do just that. They seem ready, but Jesus says to wait.

Wait for a special gift promised by Papa: a new

kind of baptism, a supernatural anointing. While John uses water, this new baptism will be with the Holy Spirit. The Holy Spirit will empower them to tell others about Jesus.

This new baptism doesn't have the tangible use of water but the intangible power of Spirit. Yet the two are connected, for the Holy Spirit shows up when John baptizes Jesus with water.

Consider John's baptism. He lowers people into the water, submerges them, and lifts them out. John's baptism symbolically parallels death, burial, and resurrection. Cleansing takes place. It's a powerful, beautiful imagery.

When Jesus emerges from the waters of his baptism, heaven opens and the Holy Spirit, in a visible form that resembles a dove, comes upon him. God's voice booms. He confirms Jesus as his son, whom he loves and whose actions he affirms. In this case, Jesus's water baptism links to the Holy Spirit. This foreshadows what is to come for his disciples with the promised gift of the Holy Spirit.

While different streams of Christianity explain the Holy Spirit's work in different ways, with varying present-day implications, we should use what happened then to inform our understanding and practices now.

Do we need to reconsider the role of the Holy Spirit in our life and our church to better align with the Bible?

[Discover more about the Holy Spirit in Acts 2:38, Acts 10:44–45, Acts 11:15–16, Acts 19:2–6, Romans 15:13, 1 Corinthians 6:19, and Jude 1:20–21.]

Today's reading comes from *Acts Bible Study: Discover How the Early Church Can Inform What We Do Today.*

DAY 24: GOD'S NEW CREATION
2 CORINTHIANS 5:11–6:2

Therefore, if anyone is in Christ, the new creation has come: The old has gone, the new is here! (2 Corinthians 5:17)

The biblical account starts with our creation in Genesis 1 and 2. After each stage of his handiwork, God proclaims the results as "good." On day six, when he fashions people—male and female, created in his image—he surveys all that he has made, and this time pronounces it as "very good" (Genesis 1:31).

Yet it may not be good enough. Here's why. In Jesus and through Jesus we can become a *new* creation, implicitly better than God's original version. If the Genesis creation was very good, what does that make us as his new creation through Jesus? How about exceptionally good?

To become God's new creation, we must believe in and follow Jesus. This transitions us from God's original creation into his new creation. But there's more. As God's new creation in Christ, the old way disappears, and a new perspective emerges. This marks our spiritual transformation.

Paul understands this well. He made a significant transformation from his old approach of harassing, hunting, and killing Jesus's followers. Replacing this he becomes a zealous follower of Christ, who endures much to encounter, convert, and instruct people about salvation through Jesus.

Like Paul, as a new creation in Jesus, our old approach to living goes away. We no longer find ourselves enslaved to sin. Though evil and the temptation to do wrong still surround us, we now comprehend them from a new perspective, one we receive in Christ and through Christ. Day by day we persevere in becoming this new creation through Jesus. We move toward perfection.

The Old Testament recognizes humanity's sins and prescribes a lengthy set of rules of what to do and not do. Yet no one can completely follow these commands. If we stumble just once, we're as guilty as if we fail every time (James 2:10).

The Old Testament ordered recurring animal sacrifices as sin offerings to address the people's shortcomings. In the New Testament, Jesus comes to fulfill the Old Testament's way. He becomes the ultimate sacrifice, the once-and-for-all payment for all sins throughout all time. Through him we can become a new creation; the old system disappears, replaced by Jesus's fresh approach.

This makes us God's new creation.

How does being a new creation in Christ affect how we live? Do our actions and attitudes prove we really believe the old is gone, and the new has come?

[Discover more about creation in Romans 1:20, Romans 8:22, Galatians 6:15, and Ephesians 1:4.]

Today's reading comes from *Love Is Patient: 40 Devotional Gems and Bible Study Truths from Paul's Letters to the Corinthians.*

DAY 25: HOLY SPIRIT POWER
ACTS 19:1 TO ACTS 20:1

When Paul placed his hands on them, the Holy Spirit came on them, and they spoke in tongues and prophesied. (Acts 19:6)

On his missionary journey, Paul heads to Ephesus. He finds a dozen believers there but is shocked that they haven't received the gift of the Holy Spirit. In fact, they don't even know who the Holy Spirit is. Paul probes a little deeper. "What baptism did you receive?"

"John's."

Paul explains that John's baptism is for repentance, preparing the way for Jesus.

Upon hearing this, the disciples want to be baptized in Jesus's name. After they are, Paul places his hands on them, and the Holy Spirit fills them. They speak in tongues and prophesy.

Next, Paul goes to the synagogue to tell his fellow Jews about Jesus, but they refuse to believe. They oppose Paul and speak against Team Jesus. Paul leaves the synagogue, taking the disciples with him. They have daily discussions in Tyrannus's lecture hall. This goes on for two years. Eventually everyone in the area hears about Jesus.

Just as the people sought healing by having Peter's shadow fall on them, God does amazing miracles through Paul too. He touches cloths, such as handkerchiefs and aprons, imparting supernatural power into them. They're taken to the sick, who are healed from their diseases, and those with evil spirits are freed.

Jesus said his followers would do even greater things than he had done once he returned to his Father. We certainly see this in Paul, as well as Peter before him.

In this new thing that God is doing in Jesus's church, we see the Holy Spirit take a central role. Holy Spirit power fills the people. The afflicted receive healing, and evil spirits are exorcised in Jesus's name. The supernatural abounds.

Some Jews invoke the name of Jesus, who Paul talks about, to cast out evil spirits. The seven sons of Sceva try this too. They don't know what they're doing. It's more supernatural power than they can handle. It backfires.

One day the evil spirit doesn't obey them. Instead, it talks back. "I know Jesus. And I know Paul. But who do you think you are?" Then the possessed man jumps them and beats all seven brothers. They run away bleeding and naked.

As word of what happened to these brothers spreads, a holy fear fills the people. They revere the name of Jesus. Many believers confess their sins. Some of those involved in sorcery show their repentance by burning all their scrolls.

Demetrius is one of the locals who opposes Paul. Though Demetrius claims this is for religious reasons, it's economic. He stirs up the people and a mob forms. After the city clerk quiets the uprising, Paul encourages the disciples, says goodbye, and leaves town.

The early church moved in supernatural power through the Holy Spirit. What can we apply from that in today's church?

[Discover more about Jesus's promise to his disciples —and us—in John 14:12–14.]

Today's reading comes from *Acts Bible Study: Discover How the Early Church Can Inform What We Do Today.*

WEEK 6: THE EMPOWERED CHURCH

DAY 26: LIVING STONES
1 PETER 2:4–8

You also, like living stones, are being built into a spiritual house to be a holy priesthood, offering spiritual sacrifices acceptable to God through Jesus Christ. (1 Peter 2:5)

Peter writes that we're built into a spiritual house as a holy priesthood to offer spiritual sacrifices (1 Peter 2:4–5). A parallel thought comes from Paul. He says that true and proper worship is to offer our bodies as living sacrifices (Romans 12:1).

First, Peter says we're living stones. As living stones, we are alive—not inanimate rocks. Jesus may have had this in mind in his rebuff of the

Pharisees who took offense at the praise his followers gave him. The teacher tells them that if the crowd doesn't celebrate his arrival, the stones will cry out to exalt him (Luke 19:39–40). To do this, the rocks would have to come alive.

As Jesus's living stones, our actions matter. We live for Jesus. We exist to honor him, praise him, and glorify him. Our purpose is to tell others about him through our actions and through our words. Our faith is alive, and what we do must show it. In doing so, we help to advance his kingdom.

Next, as living stones, we're part of God's holy temple, a spiritual house (Ephesians 2:22). We become part of the construction of his new worship space.

If we're part of his spiritual temple, we don't need to go to church to meet him. This is because, as his temple, he's already in our presence, and we're already in his. This means we can experience him at anytime, anywhere. Through Jesus, God's temple exists everywhere we go. This should give us a fresh perspective about the idea of going to church.

As living stones, we are being made into a holy priesthood. If we are truly priests through what

Jesus did for us, then we don't need ministers to point us to God, explain him to us, or assist us in encountering him. God is preparing us to do that for ourselves as his holy priests.

As living stones and holy priests, serving God in his spiritual temple, we offer to him a spiritual sacrifice. This spiritual sacrifice negates the need for the many sacrifices and offerings we read about in the Old Testament.

We are living stones built into a spiritual temple, being prepared for a holy priesthood to offer spiritual sacrifices.

This thinking is so countercultural to the way most Christians live today that it is hard for many to consider, let alone embrace. Yet through Jesus we are called to do things in a new way.

This truth can change everything—and it should.

How can we better live our lives as living stones, built into a spiritual house? How can our actions better reflect the knowledge that our bodies are temples?

[Discover more about our bodies as temples in 1 Corinthians 6:19–20.]

Today's reading comes from *1 & 2 Peter Bible Study: Practical Teaching and Profound Insights from Peter's Letters to Jesus's Church.*

DAY 27: DEALING WITH THEOLOGICAL DISAGREEMENTS
ACTS 15:1–35

Then some of the believers who belonged to the party of the Pharisees stood up and said, "The Gentiles must be circumcised and required to keep the law of Moses." (Acts 15:5)

Until now, the church has enjoyed much unity. They've gotten along, just as Jesus prayed they would. And they quickly resolved the one small, potentially divisive issue that arose about food distribution. Now they face a more challenging issue: theological disagreement. Will they overcome it, or will it cause division?

Some people from Judea show up at Antioch.

Luke doesn't tell us who these people are, and it's just as well that we don't know. They insist that the path to Jesus must be through Judaism. They specifically require the circumcision of converts, as commanded in the Law of Moses.

This isn't the first time the circumcision issue has come up. In Acts 11:1–18, this issue arose, and the church dealt with it quickly. The result was a consensus that Gentiles can be part of the church and don't have to undergo the Jewish rite of circumcision.

However, it seems that not everyone is aware of this decision, or at least they don't care about it. Some of the Pharisees who follow Jesus insist that Gentiles who want to join them must undergo circumcision and keep the Law of Moses.

The church leaders in Jerusalem get together to consider this issue—again.

Peter reminds them of his experience at Cornelius's house, when the Holy Spirit came upon the Gentiles there. As non-Jews, they weren't circumcised, and no one required them to undergo this ritual. Nor did they have to follow Jewish law. The simple requirement was that they believe in Jesus and follow him.

Then Barnabas and Paul share their experience working with Gentiles and all the supernatural things God did to bring these people into his church.

Next James, likely the brother of Jesus, speaks. He quotes the prophecy of Amos who predicted that even Gentiles would turn to God. James then summarizes his perspective that the church shouldn't add any unnecessary roadblocks for the Gentiles who want to follow Jesus.

The elders, along with the whole church, agree with James's recommendation. They draft a letter outlining their conclusion. Paul and Barnabas, accompanied by Judas (also called Barsabbas) and Silas, deliver the letter to the church in Antioch. This good news encourages the people. Judas and Silas stick around a while to help the church grow in their faith. Then they return to Jerusalem, leaving Paul and Barnabas to continue the work in Antioch.

When theological disagreements arise, do we allow them to divide us, or do we seek consensus to stay united?

[Discover more about Amos's prophecy in Amos 9:11–12.]

Today's reading comes from *Acts Bible Study: Discover How the Early Church Can Inform What We Do Today.*

DAY 28: NO DIVISIONS
1 CORINTHIANS 1:1–17

That all of you agree with one another in what you say and that there be no divisions among you, but that you be perfectly united in mind and thought. (1 Corinthians 1:10)

Paul wants the Corinthians to function as one and to live in unity—of like mind. But this unity isn't just a message for them because Paul also encourages the churches in Ephesus, Philippi, and Colossae to pursue unity with other believers. In the same way, Jesus prayed that we—his future followers—would live as one, just as he and his Father exist as one (John 17:21).

But to our shame, we divide Jesus's church. We

live in disharmony. We fight with each other over our traditions and our practices and how we comprehend God.

We spar over worship style, song selection, and a myriad of other things that relate to church practices and our perception of right living. Or to avoid these errors, we simply ignore those with other perspectives, and that's just as bad.

But the world watches us. They judge Jesus through our actions. They test what we say by the things we do. And we often fail their test.

With our words we talk about how Jesus loves everyone, but with our deeds we diminish our brothers and sisters in Christ with a holier-than-thou discord. If we can't love those in the church, how can we hope to love those outside it? We can't.

It's no wonder the world no longer respects the church of Jesus and is quick to dismiss his followers as hypocritical zealots. We brought it upon ourselves with our church splits and tens of thousands of Protestant denominations, resulting from our petty arguments over practices and theology and everything in between.

In the face of a couple of billion Christians, mostly living life contrary to God's will by not getting along with each other, what can you and I do to correct this error?

We can change this one person at a time. Find another Christian who goes to a church radically different from yours (or has dropped out of church) and embrace them as one in Christ.

If you are a mainline Christian, find a charismatic follower of Jesus and get to know him or her. If all your friends are Protestants, go to Mass and make some new friends.

If all the Christians you know look just like you, think like you, and act like you, find another Christian who is not like you. Diversify your Christian relationships to expand your understanding of what following Jesus truly looks like.

In Jesus, we are the same. It's time we embrace one another. The world is watching us to discover what we do. Instead of seeing our selfishness and sins, may they see Jesus instead.

What can we do to better live in unity with other Christians? What action can we take today?

[Discover more about unity through Jesus in Ephesians 4:3 and Philippians 4:2–3.]

Today's reading comes from *Love Is Patient: 40 Devotional Gems and Bible Study Truths from Paul's Letters to the Corinthians.*

DAY 29: BRING THEM BACK

JAMES 5:19–20

Whoever turns a sinner from the error of their way will save them from death and cover over a multitude of sins. (James 5:20)

Taken in isolation, this verse seems straightforward. It's about sharing the good news of Jesus so that people repent—that is, they stop doing what they're doing and pursue a different path to follow Jesus. Through Jesus, they will not experience eternal death but will instead experience eternal life with him. His death on the cross will cover their sins, a multitude of them.

Yet this verse isn't a call to add converts to the kingdom of God. This verse is about those who already follow Jesus.

Read the verse that precedes this one. It gives needed clarity.

James addresses "my brothers and sisters." This means they're already followers of Jesus. James writes about the possibility of one of them wandering from the truth, the truth of who Jesus is and what he did to save us.

This wandering could be anything from a short-term distraction all the way to intentionally abandoning their faith. Regardless, it seems they've walked away from Jesus.

Should we just let them go? Of course not! Someone needs to bring them back.

The person who restores them into a relationship with Jesus and his Father will save them from death and cover a multitude of sins. We could debate if this means they have backslidden or if they've lost their salvation and need to repent anew, but that distracts us from two key points in this passage.

First, we need to guard our own faith and faith practices. We must make sure we don't wander from the truth.

This can occur when we profess to following Jesus but live like the rest of the world. It can also happen when we take elements of biblical faith and add to them spiritual practices of other religions that, at their core, are contrary to Jesus and what he teaches.

Other situations that might cause us to wander from the truth are anything that produces a crisis that confronts our faith. Though we can't ensure these things won't happen, we can take precautions to minimize the chances of it occurring. We can also ask God to help us remain focused on him.

Second, we need to be ready to be the second person in this passage, the one who brings the wandering soul back to Jesus. Though the focus of many is on converts, far fewer are interested in growing disciples, which, incidentally, is what Jesus tells us to do (Matthew 28:19–20). Even fewer people give attention to those who wander off.

While James promises no tangible reward for those of us who restore someone who wanders, we can know we've done our part to keep them from death and cover their sins.

What steps can we take to make sure we don't wander from the truth of Jesus? Who has wandered away that we can help?

126

[Discover more about restoration in Galatians 6:1.]

Today's reading comes from *James & Jude Bible Study: Discover 40 Practical Insights from Jesus's Brothers.*

DAY 30: CONTEND FOR THE FAITH
JUDE 1:3–4

I felt compelled to write and urge you to contend for the faith that was once for all entrusted to God's holy people. (Jude 1:3)

Jude opens his letter with an explanation of what he wants to accomplish. Though his intention was to write about our common salvation, which he was eager to do, he changed his mind.

Instead, he feels compelled to address a different topic. He doesn't explain about this compulsion, but it's easy to perceive it as coming from the Holy Spirit's direction. What is this new topic? It's that we contend for the faith. We must endeavor to hold on to what God entrusted to us.

In contending for the faith, we strive among opposition and against difficulties. We struggle. It's like running a race that we strain to win, desiring to cross the finish line first and win our prize.

Though we might assume this struggle is against the world, it is not. It comes from within, from among followers of Jesus. Though masquerading as believers in the Messiah, they are, in fact, ungodly people. Just as certain individuals slipped into Jesus's church two thousand years ago, the same occurs today.

It should be easy to spot one ungodly person among God's holy flock, but Jude gives us two specific traits to look for.

First, they distort God's grace into a freedom to sin. More specifically, they think that Jesus's complete forgiveness grants them a license for immorality. God's grace—which gives us good things we don't deserve—is freely offered. We do not and cannot earn it. But we certainly shouldn't abuse it and assume we can live however we want, without ramifications.

Paul addresses this issue of abusing God's grace in his letter to the church in Rome. He asks rhetorically if we should persist in sin to better showcase God's grace. In case we don't know the answer, he gives it to us. "Absolutely not!" Through Jesus we have died to sin. Therefore, we should no longer live in it (Romans 6:1–2).

As Jesus's followers, sin should no longer be our master. He freed us from an impossible-to-follow law and gave us his grace instead. Therefore, we shouldn't be slaves to sin. Instead, we should pursue righteousness, that is, we should live rightly (Romans 6:11–16).

There's a second thing these ungodly people, who have infiltrated our gatherings, do. They deny Jesus's sovereignty and lordship. John also addresses this in his letter to the early believers (1 John 2:21–23). Jesus is our Lord. He died on the cross to save us, sacrificing himself to redress our sins and make us right with Father God.

If Jesus isn't who he says he is, we're foolish to follow him. Yet if Jesus is everything he claims to be, we're foolish not to.

May we guard against ungodly people who want to abuse God's grace and diminish Jesus.

When have we overrelied on God's grace? What must we do to contend for the faith and finish our race strong?

[Discover more about running our race in 1 Corinthians 9:24, Galatians 2:2, Galatians 5:7, and Hebrews 12:1.]

Today's reading comes from *James & Jude Bible Study: Discover 40 Practical Insights from Jesus's Brothers.*

WEEK 7: THE TRANSFORMED LIFE

DAY 31: LIVE FOR CHRIST
PHILIPPIANS 1

For to me, to live is Christ and to die is gain. (Philippians 1:21)

Paul reveals his perspective on life and death. It's inspiring and worthy of emulation. It's a holistic, God-centered view. In it, Paul shares his outlook for what lay ahead. It has life and death significance.

In many of his letters—including this one—Paul identifies as being a servant of Jesus Christ. This is an amazing and inspiring objective. May we adopt it as our own. As long as Paul lives, he will do so for Christ. Serving Jesus is his reason for living, life purpose, and primary goal.

As a servant of Jesus, everything Paul does is for his Savior. He tells others about Christ, encourages them to turn their lives over to Jesus, and teaches them how to grow in their faith. To Paul, Jesus matters more than anything, and all else comes after that.

In his second letter to the Corinthians, Paul details what he has suffered to serve his Savior (2 Corinthians 11:22–27). This includes being imprisoned, flogged, lashed thirty-nine times (on five separate occasions), beaten, stoned, ship-wrecked three times, often endangered, deprived of sleep, hungry and thirsty, even cold and naked.

Paul endured all this so he could boldly proclaim Jesus. He'll continue serving Jesus as long as he is alive. His labor will produce fruit for God's kingdom.

It's an awe-inspiring example that we will do well to follow.

Much later in life, Paul writes to Timothy. Paul tells his protégé that he has fought the good fight. He has finished his race. He has kept his faith (2 Timothy 4:7). Paul says he finished strong.

The alternative to life is death.

Yet Paul doesn't see death as the end. He sees it as a wonderful continuation of his existence, the culmination. In dying, Paul expects to gain even more. He anticipates living forever with Jesus. Oh, how he longs to realize that.

Paul lives in tension between continuing to serve his Savior and going to live with him forever. The first pales in comparison to the second.

Yet he acknowledges it's better for the Philippians—and implicitly many others—if he remains on earth longer. That way he can help them grow in their faith.

Life is finite, while eternal life is infinite. No matter how much life we have to live here on earth, when we die, we face an infinite existence, regardless of when we begin it.

However many days we have left, may we be like Paul and fight the good fight, finish our race, and keep our faith. May we finish strong. As we do so, let us inspire and encourage others on their faith journey.

What are we doing to live for Christ? Do we look forward to death or fear it? What do we need to focus on for the rest of our time on Earth?

[Discover people who didn't die in Genesis 5:24, 2 Kings 2:11, and possibly John 21:22–23. Read about the alternative in 1 Thessalonians 4:17.]

136

Today's reading comes from *Paul's Short Letters Bible Study: Practical Wisdom from Ten Life-Changing Epistles.*

DAY 32: ALL THINGS
ROMANS 8:18–30

We know that in all things God works for the good of those who love him, who have been called according to his purpose.
(Romans 8:28)

Today's focus verse is a favorite among many of Jesus's followers. It offers them comfort and provides encouragement amid the struggles we face. Yet, it's important to embrace the complete text.

Many shorten this sentiment to say that God works all things out for our good. But that succinct rendering skips two essential requirements.

The first is that it applies only to those who love God.

If we don't love God—Father, Son, and Holy Spirit—this promise doesn't apply to us. This love of God isn't an emotion or a feeling. It's an attitude that results in action.

We show our love to God in what we do for him, for his kingdom and his glory. Furthermore, we must love him above all others, with all our heart, soul, and mind. This is the greatest commandment (Matthew 22:36–40).

Second, it only applies to those who have been called according to his purpose.

At its basic level, God calls us to follow Jesus and live a life worthy of him. This means that loving God alone isn't enough. Yes, it's a great start, but remember that Jesus is the way to the Father; Jesus is not the destination (John 14:6).

When we are called to follow Jesus, it isn't merely for our benefit. It's to do so according to God's purpose. We shouldn't just take a onetime step toward Jesus and expect to continue living our lives as usual. This falls short of God's purpose for us.

Beyond our initial call to follow Jesus, God will call us to other things as well. We need to answer these calls and do what he wants us to do. This also is according to his purpose.

Therefore, a better recap of this verse is that when we love God and follow Jesus in obedience to what he says, our Lord will work all things out for our good.

Yet, there's more. God foreknew who would do this. He predestined them to conform to Jesus. They are called, justified, and glorified. But instead of viewing this as a succession of steps, we may be better off considering them as happening simultaneously. When we follow Jesus, we're foreknown by God, predestined, called, justified, and glorified.

With this as our framework, God will work out all things for our overall good.

Do we oversimplify this verse, like many others have? How do we show our love to God? In addition to following Jesus, what else is God calling us to do?

[Discover more about being called in 1 Corinthians 1:1, 1 Corinthians 1:9, Ephesians 1:18, 2 Thessalonians 2:14, 2 Timothy 1:9, and 1 Peter 5:10.]

Today's reading comes from *Romans Bible Study: A 40-Day Transformative Journey Through Paul's Most Powerful Letter.*

DAY 33: MAKE EVERY EFFORT
2 PETER 3:14–18

So then, dear friends, since you are looking forward to this, make every effort to be found spotless, blameless and at peace with him. (2 Peter 3:14)

Because we're looking forward to spending eternity with God in a new heaven and a new earth, Peter tells us to do three things. We don't do these, however, to get God's attention, garner his favor, or earn salvation. We've already received these three things. Instead, Peter's instructions are a response to what we already have.

First, Peter tells us to make every effort to be found spotless, that is, sinless. We are to sanctify ourselves.

Know we are already *positionally* sanctified. This happened the moment we decided to follow Jesus. Yet, our bodies are still moving in that direction to become *progressively* sanctified. This is what Peter is telling us to move toward as we await Jesus's return.

Next, Peter tells us to make every effort to be found blameless. We could view this as a repeat of being found spotless before God. But we can also look at this as encouragement to be found blameless before others. If we live a life without blame, we give others no opportunity to besmirch the name of our Savior through our bad behaviors.

Third, Peter tells us to make every effort to be at peace with Jesus. Usually when we think of living at peace, it's with other people. Yet to live at peace with Jesus reminds us to remove anything from our behavior or thinking that might cause frustration or tension toward him.

At this point in Peter's conclusion to his letter, he points out Paul's more intellectual writing style. Some of what Paul says is hard to understand, and some people distort his words. In fact, they do this with all of Scripture, which will result in their own destruction. They are both ignorant and unstable.

Since Peter has warned us, we, therefore, must be on guard to not fall victim to the same thing. We don't want to get carried away by misinterpretations of Scripture. If we do, we may fall away from our secure position in Jesus. This isn't a threat that God will take away our salvation. Jesus's promise to us is guaranteed. He will not take it back. Yet, just as we chose to follow Jesus, we could also choose to walk away. Though our position is secure from Jesus's standpoint, we have free will and can turn from him. May that never be.

As a prescription, Peter tells us to grow in grace. A simple definition of grace is to receive good things that we don't deserve. Our salvation through Jesus is a prime example of his grace. We don't deserve it, but he gives it to us anyway. His unconditional love is another example of his boundless grace. We also see his grace in many other ways.

The second of Peter's recommendations is to grow in the knowledge of Jesus Christ. As we understand Jesus more fully, we protect ourselves from the possibility of turning our backs on him.

As we grow in the grace and knowledge of Jesus, we do so for his glory. This glory occurs both now in our present world and later in heaven.

Amen.

What can we do to make every effort to be found spotless, blameless, and at peace with Jesus? How can we better grow in the grace and knowledge of our Savior?

[Discover more about God's grace in John 1:17, Acts 15:11, Romans 3:22–24, 1 Corinthians 1:4, and 2 Timothy 1:9.]

Today's reading comes from *1 & 2 Peter Bible Study: Practical Teaching and Profound Insights from Peter's Letters to Jesus's Church.*

DAY 34: NOTHING CAN SEPARATE US
ROMANS 8:31–39

Who shall separate us from the love of Christ? Shall trouble or hardship or persecution or famine or nakedness or danger or sword? (Romans 8:35)

Paul asks if anyone can separate us from Jesus's love. This may be a rhetorical question, but even if it isn't, we know that nothing can separate us from Jesus's love. He did, after all, come to Earth to die in our place as the ultimate sin sacrifice for all the wrong things we have done—and will ever do.

That's the epitome of love. Therefore, no one will ever be able to come between us and his love for us.

People can cause us great trouble. They can attack us, torment us, verbally assault us. Through it all, Jesus loves us.

We can endure hardship brought about by others. They can take what is ours. They can repress us. And they can abandon us when we're in need. Jesus never will. His love for us will continue through it all.

Next is persecution. When we follow Jesus, people may persecute us for our faith and how we put our faith into action. This goes beyond facing trouble or enduring hardship. Though the persecution could be verbal, it could also be physical. Jesus stands with us through it all. His love never wavers.

Consider famine. When we're hungry and lack the food we need, Jesus loves us amid our suffering.

If we're naked or need clothes to cover us, Jesus is there with us.

If we face danger, Jesus stands by us.

If our life is threatened, Jesus remains with us. And even if our life is taken, we will spend eternity with our Savior.

Through all these things, we can overcome them through Jesus and his love for us.

Yet Paul has more to share.

Neither death nor life will separate us from Jesus's love.

Angels can't interrupt Jesus's love, and demons are powerless to oppose it.

Nothing in our present reality and nothing in our future will separate us from Jesus.

Neither will any power come between us and Jesus's love. This includes both those with worldly power and those with supernatural power.

Last, we know that some people are afraid of heights, and others fear depths, either in the water or underground. Yet in both situations, Jesus's love is there with us.

In fact, nothing in all of creation will ever be able to separate us from God's great love for us that is manifest in Jesus our Lord.

Which items on this list do we struggle with the most to accept? Knowing that nothing can separate us from Jesus's love, is there anything that we should fear? What should our response be to Jesus's love?

[Discover more about Jesus's love for us in 2 Thessalonians 2:16–17 and 1 John 3:16.]

Today's reading comes from *Romans Bible Study: A 40-Day Transformative Journey Through Paul's Most Powerful Letter.*

DAY 35: DEVOTED TO JESUS
2 CORINTHIANS 11:1–33

But I am afraid that just as Eve was deceived by the serpent's cunning, your minds may somehow be led astray from your sincere and pure devotion to Christ. (2 Corinthians 11:3)

In 1 Corinthians 15:22 we see Paul placing the blame for humanity's fall on Adam. In the above passage, however, Paul focuses on Eve's role in the couple's disobedience to their creator's command. He says plainly that the serpent's cunning deceived Eve.

Paul worries that in the same way the church in Corinth might also diverge from their faith—that they'll go astray by following the wrong influences of others, thereby ditching their devotion to Jesus.

He doesn't share the source of this deception. But the threat could arise from false teachers who misrepresent Jesus, the devil's cunning schemes, or both.

Paul fears this outcome for the church in Corinth. This is despite the eighteen months he spent with them, a subsequent visit, his prayers, and his letters of instruction to them. He has invested much into them, yet he's afraid they'll veer off track. If, after all this, Paul carries this unease about them, we too should guard against influences that could lead us astray.

This isn't an issue of them walking away from their faith. Instead, Paul is concerned that these negative influences will detract from their "sincere and pure devotion" to Jesus.

The word devotion only occurs one other time in the New Testament. You might already suspect where. It appears in Paul's other letter to his friends in Corinth. This time he urges them to live with an "undivided devotion to the Lord" (1 Corinthians 7:35).

Merging these two related verses, we get a sense that our devotion to Jesus should be sincere, pure, and undivided. The opposite of this is insincere, impure, and divided. This gives us a sense of incomplete devotion, a partial commitment to following Jesus. It's unacceptable.

When we believe in Jesus and follow him, he wants us to go all in. There is no looking back (Genesis 19:23–26 and Luke 9:62). God deserves our complete devotion for the rest of our lives. We must reject anything or anyone that distracts us from him.

Are we fully devoted to Jesus, or only partially so? What influences must we remove from our life that threaten to distract us from our dedication to our Savior?

[Discover more about devotion to Jesus in Matthew 6:24, Hebrews 10:36–39, and 1 John 1:6–7.]

Today's reading comes from *Love Is Patient: 40 Devotional Gems and Bible Study Truths from Paul's Letters to the Corinthians.*

WEEK 8: THE COMING KING

DAY 36: RUN WITH PERSEVERANCE
HEBREWS 12:1–3

Let us run with perseverance the race marked out for us, fixing our eyes on Jesus, the pioneer and perfecter of faith.
(Hebrews 12:1–2)

Today's passage opens with the word *therefore*. *Therefore* connects what follows it with what precedes it. In this case it's our Hebrews 11 hall of faith.

It provides us with the imagery of a great cloud of witnesses surrounding us, people of noteworthy faith. We can interpret their witness in two ways. One is that their lives serve as a witness to us. The other is that they are witnessing *our* lives. Imagine these Old Testament Saints watching us and cheering us on as we move down our journey of faith. It's a heady thought. May we find encouragement in it.

Because of their example and their witness, the writers of Hebrews encourage us to do two things. Both begin with the inspiring instruction of "let us."

First, the text says to let us throw off everything that holds us back, to jettison each weight that slows us down. This includes the entanglement of sin. If we wrongly hold on to these things, it does not negate our right standing with Jesus, but it does affect how we live our lives while we're here on earth and the reward we'll receive once we leave this place. Remember, we have an impressive throng of witnesses cheering us on.

Second, let us run with perseverance the race before us. Having ridden ourselves of all the baggage that would slow us down, we're ready to run. We are poised to speed down the path God has for us. As we do, we want to keep our focus on Jesus, to maintain a steady gaze on him. He is the reason for our faith and the perfecter of it.

Jesus now sits in heaven at God's right hand. He, too, is our witness. His life and sacrifice serve as a witness to us. And, from the vantage of heaven, he witnesses what we're doing with this new life that he gave us.

If the patriarchs' witness motivates us to move forward in faith, how much more should Jesus's witness? He endured for us, which should encourage us to persevere for him, to not grow weary or lose heart.

We must, therefore, run our race with perseverance.

How can we best run our race with perseverance? How can Jesus and the great cloud of witnesses encourage us in our faith journey?

[Discover more about perseverance in Romans 5:1–4, James 1:2–4, and 2 Peter 1:5–7.]

Today's reading comes from *Hebrews Bible Study: A 40-Day Exploration of Faith, Perseverance, and Godly Living.*

DAY 37: FINISH STRONG
2 TIMOTHY 3–4

I have fought the good fight, I have finished the race, I have kept the faith. (2 Timothy 4:7)

In our introduction to Paul's second letter to Timothy, we noted it reads like a last will and testament. It also gives final instructions to Timothy, so we shouldn't be surprised with today's verse.

Paul realizes his time to depart this earth approaches (2 Timothy 4:6). Toward this end, he says he's being poured out like a drink offering. He also mentions this to the Philippian church (Philippians 2:17).

A drink offering is first described in the book of Genesis. It's Jacob's response to his encounter with God (Genesis 35:14). Visually, once poured out, the drink offering is given irrevocably. Paul sees this happening in his own life. He's completely giving everything to tell others about Jesus.

With his approaching death in view, Paul anticipates his future. He sees a crown of righteousness awaiting him, which Jesus will award to him—and to all of us (2 Timothy 4:8).

From this perspective, Paul summarizes his life from the vantage point that he is about to die. He fought well, finished his race, and kept the faith.

As Paul wraps up his first letter to Timothy, he uses similar language, encouraging Timothy to fight the good fight of faith (1 Timothy 6:12). Now Paul affirms he did exactly what he told Timothy to do. He fought the good fight. How this must encourage Timothy, knowing that his mentor accomplished one of the things he instructed his protégé to do.

Though we may not think of our life with Jesus as being a good fight, recall that our battle isn't physical but spiritual (Ephesians 6:12). Our enemy opposes us, and we must fight against him (1 Peter 5:8). When we do, we fight the good fight.

Next, Paul confirms he finished his race. He ran well and crossed the finish line. He did what God told him to do. Paul often uses the analogy of running a race in his letters (1 Corinthians 9:24 and Galatians 5:7).

Earlier in his ministry, Paul checked with other leaders of Jesus's church to make sure he was running in the right direction, that he was not running in vain (Galatians 2:2). Affirmed that he was on the right track, Paul persevered in his race.

Last, he kept the faith—that is, his faith in Jesus. Paul writes about faith in each of his letters. He says he lives by faith (Galatians 2:20). He talks about the unity of faith (Ephesians 4:13). And he writes about a shield of faith, which protects against the enemy's flaming arrows (Ephesians 6:16).

Let us be like Paul and finish our race strong. How we start life doesn't matter, but how we end matters more than anything.

How are we doing at fighting the good fight? Are we on track to finish our race? Are we keeping the faith? How committed are we to finishing strong?

[Discover more about Paul's outlook on his life in Acts 20:24.]

Today's reading comes from *Paul's Short Letters Bible Study: Practical Wisdom from Ten Life-Changing Epistles*.

DAY 38: THE REVELATION OF JESUS
REVELATION 1:1–3

The revelation from Jesus Christ, which God gave him to show his servants what must soon take place. (Revelation 1:1)

We think of the book of Revelation as John's revelation, but, in fact, it is Jesus's. John is only the recipient. This revelation comes from Jesus. Father God gave it to him. Jesus shares this revelation with John through a supernatural vision as the apostle communes with God in the spiritual realm (Revelation 1:10).

An angel shows up in John's vision to reveal Jesus's revelation. The intent of the vision—that is, the revelation—is to show John what will soon take place.

As we comprehend time, we can easily conclude that *soon* has already occurred, since we are now 2,000 years distant from John's recording of these words. Yet we must acknowledge that God views time differently than we do. A thousand years to us are but a day to him and a day to us may be a thousand years to him (Psalm 90:4 and 2 Peter 3:8).

So when we read John's words that the time is near, this shouldn't perplex us. If we literally equate 2,000 years of our time to two days for God, then we are but two days removed from this revelation. In this respect, we can accept that the time is, indeed, quite near.

Yet a literal application of Scripture's statement about God's view of time may be an overreach. The principle to grasp, however, is that we comprehend time much differently than God. Given this, we can accept that these events will soon take place because the time is near, even though those words took place two millennia ago. Time isn't a problem for God, only for us.

John confirms that his vision is a prophecy. In a delightful simplicity, we'll receive God's blessing by merely reading it, hearing it, and taking it to heart (Revelation 1:3). Don't miss this point.

John doesn't say we need to understand what it says. Just like the rest of Scripture, we can now only know in part. Rather, we should read it and be amazed. That's the intent. And God will bless us when we do.

Beyond that we find another hint at the purpose of John's vision much later in Revelation. The aim of Revelation may be simply to worship God and celebrate Jesus (Revelation 19:10).

How well do we accept that we understand time differently than God? How content are we to read, hear, and take to heart the book of Revelation?

[Discover what else John says about Jesus and how it relates to our view of time in John 1:1–5.]

Today's reading comes from *Revelation Bible Study: Discover Practical Insights from John's Epic Vision.*

DAY 39: THE ALPHA AND OMEGA
REVELATION 22:12–16

"I am the Alpha and the Omega, the First and the Last, the Beginning and the End." (Revelation 22:13)

This passage in Revelation records Jesus's words, and it's his final teaching in the Bible. As such, it deserves our careful attention.

Jesus comes with his reward, to give each person what they deserve based on what they've done. This comes as a surprising declaration, implying that we'll receive salvation through our actions.

Aren't we saved by grace through faith? Yes, we are. Isn't salvation a gift that we can't earn? Yes, it is (Ephesians 2:8–9).

Then why will Jesus look at what we've done? Though we may remember our many sins and cringe with shame at the recollection, God blots out the sins of those who follow him, remembering them no more (Isaiah 43:25). Through him we have a clean slate.

This means that God's record of what we've done is far different than our own recollection. To him we are his pure, spotless bride (Ephesians 5:27). When we follow Jesus, we need not wallow in worry over our past mistakes because through him we are made right (Romans 5:19).

This restored standing gives us the right to eat from the tree of life. We may enter the new Jerusalem through the city gates where we'll become Jesus's bride. Nothing impure will be able to enter (Revelation 21:27).

Yet not all will have this confidence when they see Jesus coming at the end of time. He says that the practitioners of magic arts, the sexually immoral, murderers, and idolaters, along with all who persist in lying will remain on the outside looking in. He'll bar their entrance into the new Jerusalem.

Does this list sound familiar?

God gave a similar itemization in Revelation 21. God's list is a bit longer, but he includes everything Jesus mentions. The people who do these things will end up in the fiery lake that burns with sulfur. This is the second death (Revelation 21:8).

In his message, Jesus also reveals some names for himself. He is the Root of David, as well as his Offspring, both preceding and following Israel's second king. Jesus is the bright Morning Star. And Jesus is the Alpha and the Omega. That is, he is the First and the Last, the Beginning and the End.

This is a reminder that just as Jesus is present here in Revelation at the end of time, he was also present at the beginning of creation (Genesis 1:26 and John 1:1–4). Through him we are, and through him we will be. He created our physical bodies, and he saves our spiritual selves.

Are we still holding on to the sins that Jesus has already forgiven and forgotten? How can we better respond to Jesus as the Alpha and Omega?

[Discover more about the Alpha and Omega, the First and the Last, in Revelation 1:8, 1:17, 2:8, and

21:6. Read more about the morning star in 2 Peter 1:19 and Revelation 2:28.]

Today's reading comes from *Revelation Bible Study: Discover Practical Insights from John's Epic Vision.*

DAY 40: COMING SOON
REVELATION 22:17–21

He who testifies to these things says, "Yes, I am coming soon." (Revelation 22:20)

After Jesus finishes his last teaching in the book of Revelation, the Holy Spirit weighs in as well. But it's not just him. It's also the bride (not the bridegroom). This means you and me, all whose names appear in the Lamb's book of life. We join with the Holy Spirit to bid people to "Come!" And everyone who hears our offer we'll add to the invitation and likewise say to others, "Come!"

This invite is to anyone who's thirsty. They may come to him. Anyone who wants to can receive

Jesus's no-strings-attached gift of living water. Isn't this exciting?

Only a few verses ago, in Revelation 22:11, it seemed too late for those who hadn't already decided to follow Jesus. But now it feels as though they're given one last, final chance. The invitation, given three times, is to come to Jesus and receive the water of life.

We serve a God of second chances. And third chances. And even more than we can count. He is patient because he wants as many to come to him as possible (2 Peter 3:9).

But we need to come to Jesus before it's too late, perhaps before he returns, which will happen soon.

In this chapter in Revelation, Jesus speaks three times.

The first is in verse 7. Then comes his longer message (which we just covered) in verses 12 through 16. His final words in all of Scripture appear at the end of verse 20.

In each of these three passages he repeats the same phrase: "I am coming soon."

This threefold testimony from Jesus that he's coming soon repeats to underscore its importance. Though Jesus saying it once is enough, saying it twice adds emphasis, while three times confirms beyond all doubt that it will happen.

Yet we must acknowledge that God reckons time differently than we do. What is *soon* to him may not be *soon* to us. Indeed, 2,000 years ago Jesus told his followers that his kingdom was near, that it was coming soon. The early church understood this as meaning any day, just as many people now make the same assumption.

As Jesus's followers, how can we understand his promise that he is coming soon? How should we live our lives in this tension between him coming soon and having already waited two millennia?

We must embrace both scenarios.

We should strive to simultaneously expect that he's coming back today and seek to live every day for the rest of our lives to advance his kingdom and raise up future generations to follow him too. We should balance the seemingly competing realities that he is coming soon *and* that we may die before he does.

Since Jesus could come any day, what are we doing to make each remaining moment count? And as we wait, what are we doing to produce a long-term kingdom impact?

[Discover more about Jesus coming soon in Hebrews 10:36–37, Revelation 2:16, and Revelation 3:11. Read about the kingdom of God (heaven) being near in Matthew 3:2, Mark 1:15, and Luke 21:31.]

Today's reading comes from *Revelation Bible Study: Discover Practical Insights from John's Epic Vision.*

If you liked *Discovering Jesus,* please leave a review online. Your review will help others discover this book and encourage them to read it too.

Thank you.

THE 40-DAY BIBLE STUDY SERIES

Which book do you want to read in the 40-Day
Bible Study Series?

- Dear Theophilus (the Gospel of Luke)
- Acts Bible Study
- Isaiah Bible Study
- Minor Prophets Bible Study
- Job Bible Study
- Living Water (John)
- Love Is Patient (1 and 2 Corinthians)
- Revelation Bible Study
- 1, 2, & 3 John Bible Study
- Hebrews Bible Study
- James and Jude Bible Study
- Matthew Bible Study

- 1 & 2 Peter Bible Study
- Mark Bible Study
- Romans Bible Study
- Paul's Short Epistles Bible Study

For a list of all Peter's books, go to PeterDeHaan.com/nonfiction.

FOR SMALL GROUPS, SUNDAY SCHOOL, AND CLASSES

Discovering Jesus makes an ideal eight-week Bible study discussion guide for small groups, Sunday School, and classes. To prepare for the conversation, read one chapter of this book each weekday, Monday through Friday.

- Week 1: The Promised Word
- Week 2: The Earthly Ministry
- Week 3: The Radical Call of Discipleship
- Week 4: The Ultimate Sacrifice
- Week 5: The Risen Lord and His Spirit
- Week 6: The Empowered Church
- Week 7: The Transformed Life
- Week 8: The Coming King

When you get together, discuss the questions at the end of each chapter. The leader can use all the questions to guide this discussion or pick which ones to focus on.

Before beginning the discussion, pray as a group. Ask for Holy Spirit insight and clarity.

As you consider each chapter's questions:

- Look at how this can grow your understanding of the Bible.
- Evaluate how this can expand your faith perspective.
- Consider what you need to change in how you live your lives.

End by asking God to help apply what you've learned.

May God bless you as you read and study his Word.

ABOUT THE BIBLE

Each entry in this book contains Bible references. These can guide you if you want to learn more. If you're not familiar with the Bible, here's an overview to get you started, give some context, and minimize confusion.

First, the Bible is a collection of works written by various authors over several centuries. Think of the Bible as a diverse anthology of godly communication. It contains historical accounts, poetry, songs, letters of instruction and encouragement, messages from God sent through his representatives, and prophecies.

Most versions of the Bible have sixty-six books grouped into two sections: the Old Testament and the New Testament. The Old Testament contains thirty-nine books that precede and anticipate Jesus. The New Testament includes twenty-seven books and covers Jesus's life and the work of his followers.

The reference notations in the Bible, such as Romans 3:23, are analogous to line numbers in a Shakespearean play. They serve as a study aid. Since the Bible is much longer and more complex than a play, its reference notations are more involved.

As already mentioned, the Bible is an amalgam of books, or sections, such as Genesis, Psalms, or Matthew. These are the names given to them, over time, based on the piece's author, audience, or purpose.

In the 1200s, each book was divided into chapters, such as Acts 2 or Psalm 23. In the 1500s, the chapters were further subdivided into verses, such as John 3:16. Let's use this as an example.

The name of the book (John) appears first, followed by the chapter number (3), a colon, and then the verse number (16). Sometimes called a chapter-verse reference notation, this helps people quickly find a specific text regardless of their version of the Bible.

Although the goal was to place these chapter and verse divisions at logical breaks, they sometimes seem arbitrary. Therefore, it's good practice to read what precedes and follows each passage you're studying. The text before or after it may contain relevant insights into the portion you're exploring.

Here's how to look up a specific passage in the Bible based on its reference: Most Bibles contain a table of contents, which gives the page number for the beginning of each book. Start there. Locate the book you want to read, and turn to that page. Then flip forward to the chapter you want. Last, skim that chapter to locate the specific verse.

If you want to read online, enter the reference into BibleGateway.com or BibleHub.com. Also check out the YouVersion app.

Learn more about the greatest book ever written at ABibleADay.com, which provides a Bible blog, summaries of the books of the Bible, a dictionary of Bible terms, Bible reading plans, and other resources.

ABOUT PETER DEHAAN

Peter DeHaan, PhD, wants to change the world one word at a time. His books and blog posts discuss God, the Bible, and church, geared toward spiritual seekers and church dropouts. Many people feel church has let them down, and Peter seeks to encourage them as they search for a place to belong.

But he's not afraid to ask tough questions or make religious people squirm. He's not trying to be provocative. Instead, he seeks truth, even if it makes people uncomfortable. Peter urges Christians to push past the status quo and reexamine how they practice their faith in every part of their lives.

Peter earned his doctorate, awarded with high distinction, from Trinity College of the Bible and Theological Seminary. He lives with his wife in beautiful Southwest Michigan and wrangles crossword puzzles in his spare time.

A lifelong student of Scripture, Peter wrote the 1,000-page website ABibleADay.com to encourage people to explore the Bible, the greatest book ever written. His popular blog addresses biblical Christianity to build a faith that matters.

Read his blog, receive his newsletter, and learn more at PeterDeHaan.com.

BOOKS BY PETER DEHAAN

40-DAY BIBLE STUDY SERIES

Dear Theophilus (the Gospel of Luke)

Acts Bible Study

Isaiah Bible Study

Minor Prophets Bible Study

Job Bible Study

Living Water (John)

Love Is Patient (1 and 2 Corinthians)

Revelation Bible Study

1, 2, & 3 John Bible Study

Hebrews Bible Study

James and Jude Bible Study

Matthew Bible Study

1 & 2 Peter Bible Study

Mark Bible Study

Romans Bible Study

Paul's Short Epistles Bible Study

HOLIDAY CELEBRATION DEVOTIONALS

The Advent of Jesus

The Passion of Jesus (Lent)

The Victory of Jesus (Easter)

The Ministry of Jesus

Thanksgiving with Jesus

New Year with Jesus

BIBLE CHARACTER SKETCHES SERIES

Women of the Bible

The Friends and Foes of Jesus

Old Testament Sinners and Saints

More Old Testament Sinners and Saints

Heroes and Heavies of the Apocrypha

200 Old Testament Sinners and Saints

VISITING CHURCHES SERIES

52 Churches

The 52 Churches Workbook

More Than 52 Churches

The More Than 52 Churches Workbook

Visiting Online Church

Shopping for Church

OTHER BOOKS

Elephant God

Jesus's Broken Church

Martin Luther's 95 Theses (formerly *95 Tweets*)

The Christian Church's LGBTQ Failure

Bridging the Sacred-Secular Divide (formerly *Woodpecker Wars*)

Beyond Psalm 150

For the latest list of all Peter's books, go to PeterDeHaan.com/nonfiction.